Accession no.

D0414781

STUDYING FILMS

ALSO AVAILABLE IN THIS SERIES

Studying Blade Runner

Sean Redmond

Studying Chungking Express

Sean Redmond

Studying City of God

Stephanie Muir

Studying Disaster Movies

John Sanders

Studying The Matrix

Anna Dawson

Studying Surrealist and Fantasy Cinema

Neil Coombs

Studying Tsotsi

Judith Gunn

FORTHCOMING

Studying Bollywood

Garret Fay

Studying Pan's Labyrinth

Tanya Jones

STUDYING THE DEVIL'S BACKBONE

(El espinazo del diablo)

James Rose

LIS LIBRARY

Date	Fund
14.5.2010	pt 791.4372 ROS
Order No	
02113417	
University of Chester	

36121763

auteur

Acknowledgements

The author would like to thank Claire Robinson for her insightful comments regarding ghosts, orphans and explosions. A big thank you to Neil Smith and Scott Langford for their support and humour in getting me through it all. Thanks once again to John Atkinson at Auteur for his support, encouragement and advice and to Helen Rose for putting up with it all again.

Dedication

For my parents, who have consistently supported and encouraged me since the beginning.

First published in 2009 by
Auteur, The Old Surgery, 9 Pulford Road, Leighton Buzzard LU7 1AB
www.auteur.co.uk
Copyright © Auteur 2009

Series design: Nikki Hamlett
Cover image © BFI Stills, Posters and Designs
All DVD framegrabs taken from the Region 2 DVD edition of *The Devil's Backbone* available from Optimum Home Entertainment.
Set by AMP Ltd, Dunstable, Bedfordshire
Printed and bound in Poland; produced by Polskabook

All rights reserved. No part of this publication may be reproduced in any material form (including photocopying or storing in any medium by electronic means and whether or not transiently or incidentally to some other use of this publication) without the permission of the copyright owner.

British Library Cataloguing-in-Publication Data
A catalogue record for this book is available from the British Library

ISBN 978-1-906733-09-4

Contents

Studying *The Devil's Backbone* Factsheet 6

1. Guillermo del Toro 7

2. Narrative 19

3. Character Outlines 39

4. Elements, Themes and Motifs 67

5. Film Language – Focused Scene Analysis 87

Appendix 97

Guillermo del Toro Chronology 99

Extended Bibliography and Filmography 103

Factsheet

The Devil's Backbone (El espinazo del diablo)

	2001, Mexico/Spain
Running Time	108 minutes
Certificate	'R' in America and '15' in UK
Production Companies	El Deseo, S.A. and Tequila Gang
Distributor	Sony Pictures Classics

Key credits

Director	Guillermo del Toro
Written by	Guillermo del Toro, Antonio Trashorras and David Muñoz
Producer	Augustín Almodóvar and Bertha Navarro
Director of Photography	Guillermo Navarro
Music by	Javier Navarrete
Editor	Luis De la Madrid

Cast

Carmen	Marisa Paredes	Jaime	Ínigo Garcés
Jacinto	Eduardo Noriega	Conchita	Irene Visedo
Casares	Federico Luppi	Santi	Junio Valverde
Carlos	Fernando Tielve		

Honours and Awards

Winner: International Critics Award/Special Jury Prize/Youth Jury Grand Prize Gérardmer Film Festival 2002

Winner: Méliès D'Argent Amsterdam Fantastic Film Festival 2002

Synopsis

Spain. The Civil War is steadily being won by the Nationalists. In an isolated orphanage in the Spanish Plain, ten-year-old Carlos discovers the presence of a ghost, a spectre the other boys call *The One who sighs*. Although frightened, Carlos begins an investigation into establishing who the ghost is and what it wants. His enquiries lead him into trouble with the orphanage bully Jaime and the equally violent Jacinto, the orphanage caretaker. Whilst Carlos investigates the ghost, the adults who look after the children are revealed to be involved in unsettled relationships, particularly Jacinto and Carmen, the orphanage governess. Whilst Carmen is using Jacinto for sex, Jacinto is using Carmen to obtain the keys to the orphanage safe. Inside, there is a stash of Republican gold, gold which Jacinto intends to steal. As the film draws towards its end, Jaime confesses to Carlos that he witnessed Jacinto accidentally kill a boy called Santi and it is his restless spirit that haunts the orphanage. With this knowledge, Carlos confronts the ghost by name and asks what it wants. The spectre replies that it wants Jacinto in order to avenge his murder. Before Carlos can act upon this request, Jacinto, in a fit of rage, blows up the orphanage, killing Carmen and the other teachers. Rounding up the surviving orphans, Jacinto makes the boys look for the safe. Once they find it he locks them up, intending to leave them to starve to death. As he gathers up the gold, Jaime and Carlos band together with the other boys and escape. Armed with wooden stakes, the boys attack Jacinto and force him into the ghost's lair where upon the dead child embraces the man and drags him deep under water and so drowns him. The film concludes with the surviving boys walking out of the orphanage and into the Spanish Plain.

Budget

US$4,500,00 (est.)

GUILLERMO DEL TORO

Born 9 October 1964 in Guadalajara, Jalsico, Mexico.

Early Film-making

Del Toro's first cinematic efforts started when he was a child: shooting on Super 8, he would film battles between his *Planet of the Apes* and Universal Monsters toys. By his own admission these films were 'quite violent' and used 'lots of ketchup and not much production values' (del Toro, 2006). These first ventures into film steadily developed: by the age of 15 his film-making practice had become more complex as he had begun to organise his friends into cast and crew. With this support del Toro would make films that were scaled by the length of time they took to make: 'we called [complex productions] two afternoons and less complex productions which were [called] an afternoon or half an afternoon' (ibid.). Out of these experiences emerged his first shorts:

> My mother was my actress in two short films... One was called *Geometria* which was in the 1980s. She suffered a brutal death at the hands of a zombie who tore her eye

out and bit her neck... Before that she acted in an even more bizarre short called *Matilde*. It was about a woman who has a psycho-sexual obsession with a crack in the wall of her bedroom out of which emerges a gigantic blind foetus which is herself and which strangles her. A profoundly abnormal story but entertaining. (ibid.)

Whilst these fledgling film-making activities enabled the young del Toro to not only learn the basic technical skills of film production and direction, they more importantly fostered his burgeoning imagination and his immense sense of creativity. Although this suggests that del Toro's childhood formed an invaluable part of his development into a 'visionary'[1] director, it was to do so at the expense of the other, non-film-making related experiences he also had as a child: in interviews or during DVD commentaries, del Toro often engages in autobiographical revelation, citing the cause of stories, scenes or images in his films as something seen or experienced during his childhood. Such instances seem to have had a profound effect and marked his cinematic output indelibly by constructing his sympathies with the monster or suggesting aspects of their design, by defining character relationships, or providing the painfully realistic details within some of the violent moments of his films. For example, when discussing his debut, *Cronos* (1993), he has stated that it is 'sort of autobiographical [being based upon] my relationship with my grandmother which was difficult but very full of love in which we both forgave each other our imperfections' (ibid.) or during his DVD commentary for *Pan's Labyrinth* (2006) he reflects on the detail of the moment when Captain Vidal repeatedly smashes a young man's face with a bottle by saying that the fact that the bottle does not break came from an incident when he was involved in a street brawl – while he was on the ground being beaten with a chain, he watched as his friend was repeatedly hit with a bottle, commenting that despite the pain he was feeling, he noticed that the bottle didn't break upon his friend's head, regardless of the force being used. This aspect of del Toro integrating the moments and details of his past into his cinema is greatly amplified in *The Devil's Backbone* (2001), with del Toro stating that 'the beauty of *The Devil's Backbone* for me personally is that it is incredibly autobiographical. Many of the things that happen in the movie happened to me in obviously a different way' (del Toro, 2004). Of these many moments, the one that dominates relates to a family member, del Toro's uncle Guillermo:

> He and I were very good friends. He introduced me to horror literature and horror films... he died young but about a year or two before he died he said to me 'When I die, I'll come back and let you know if there's something out there.' I inherited his room, his books and everything. While I was in his room, watching TV, I started hearing him sigh, really sadly, and for twenty minutes, like the kid in the movie, instead of being afraid I investigated what it could have been. Then I realized it was an honest-to-goodness disembodied voice floating about half a foot from my face, and I realized who it was in a flash of introspection. I left, and I never came back to that room. But to this day, I'm absolutely certain I investigated everything with enough calm to tell you that was a ghost. That was a voice. It was not an air draft. It was nothing logical. (Chun, n.d.)

This supernatural incident forms the basis for Santi, the ghost of *The Devil's Backbone*: when the manifestations begin it is simply the sound of sighing, a soft breath heard by the children as they lie awake in their dormitory. Carlos, the child protagonist, like del Toro, is not afraid and calmly investigates the dark corridors when he hears the sound.

His inquisitiveness leads him to the cistern where Santi was murdered and, by stepping into that space, unwittingly makes an unspoken pact with the ghost. From then on, the living boy and the dead child are bound, with Carlos soon realising who Santi is and why he is haunting the orphanage corridors.

Other biographical moments relate to the design of the classroom in which the orphans study as it is a close recreation of the school room in which del Toro was taught; and the scene in which Carlos is 'branded a squealer' (ibid.) was an incident from his childhood. Other self-referential moments include:

> The excursion for water happened to me and my brothers when we used to sleep in my grandmother's house. It was a big old Mexican house with a gigantic patio in the centre and we had to go fetch water from the kitchen. We had to cross the empty patio at night with out little glasses of water. At night, when you're a child, [its] a space full of noises, full of presence…

> I have always dreaded this moment in my grandmother's house. That moment when I would turn a corner in one of those long corridors that were in the house which was,

by the way, very much titled like this corridor, I would discover somebody. Just a silhouette at the end of the corridor. This was one of my early nightmares as a child. To see it re-enacted here is a pure act of exorcism. (ibid.)

Linking many of these events is the figure of del Toro's 'grandmother'.

Del Toro's 'Grandmother'

During his childhood, del Toro spent a lot of his time with a woman he calls 'grandmother'. This woman was not his biological grandparent – she had died during childbirth – but his grandmother's sister. A strong and devout Catholic, del Toro's grandmother 'basically' (Romney, 2006) raised him. He has commented that she was a very scary woman but someone who loved him deeply. From this opposition arose two arresting moments for del Toro: in one interview the director describes how she would force him to walk to school with upturned bottle caps in his shoes, 'knowing the pain would be a small down payment on everlasting peace' (DePalma, 1994). Del Toro then goes on to explain that when he was 13 he wandered down to the morgue of a municipal hospital 'where he saw a pile of discarded foetuses. I understood right then there was no God' (ibid.). From that point on he became 'a raging atheist' (ibid.) which turned his surrogate grandmother against him and resulted in his exorcism:

She exorcised me twice – with holy water, literally. The more holy water she threw at me, the more ridiculous I thought it was, and I was laughing harder, and of course she was shitting in her pants, it was so scary for her. (Romney, 2006)

Del Toro continues by describing the last time he saw her:

> I showed her some of my sculptures and my drawings and she started crying. She was very feeble, she had had a stroke, and she said, 'Why could you never do a beautiful thing?' I said, 'These are beautiful things'. (ibid.)

Film Education

Del Toro studied screenwriting with Mexican film director Jaime Humberto Hermosillo at the University of Guadalajara. During this time, del Toro would write the first drafts of *The Devil's Backbone*. At that point the narrative was set during the Mexican Revolution but the symbolic and metaphoric values del Toro was trying to communicate did not successfully synthesise with that political struggle. Del Toro continued to work on the screenplay and eventually submitted the final draft to Hermosillo as his graduation thesis. According to del Toro, 'Hermosillo was very strict on presentation and formatting and didn't like the way the script was formatted... He took it and threw it in the garbage, telling me that he will not read it until I learn to present my stuff more cleanly... Looking back, it was not such a big loss because *The Devil's Backbone* evolved into a better movie.' (Wood, 2006: 32-3)

After graduation del Toro attended Dick Smith's[2] Advanced Make-up course where he learnt the art of special effects make-up. From there he formed his own effects company, *Necropia*, which would go on to garner great success and allow del Toro to begin his move into writing, producing and directing. His first foray into professional film-making was to produce the gay romantic comedy *Doña Herlinda y su hijo* (*Dona Herlinda and Her Son*, 1985) with Manuel Barbachano Ponce. The film was written and directed by his University tutor Hermosillo and starred del Toro's mother, Guadalupe del Toro (who also financed the film), in the title role.

With this experience and the success of *Necropia*, del Toro began to write and then direct episodes of *Hora Marcada* (*The Appointed Time*), (1986 – 1990) a Mexican horror anthology television show. During this period, del Toro began to write what would become his debut feature, *Cronos* (1993): a startlingly unique vampire film, it has won over 25 international awards[3], including the Critics Prize at Cannes. The film concerns an aging antique dealer, Jesus Gris, who finds a gold Faberge-like egg in the base of a religious statue. At first he believes it to be a clockwork toy which he winds up and rests in the palm of his hand: but six 'legs' spring out of the side of the egg and embed themselves into Jesus' hand, simultaneously sucking his blood and transferring vampiric venom into him. As the story unfolds, Jesus becomes addicted to the bite of the egg and steadily transforms into a vampire, shedding his aging skin as he grows immortal and seeking out fresh blood to slake his insatiable thirst.

The value of the film lies not only in the director's treatment of the vampire myth (here the source vampire is an ancient insect contained within a clockwork mechanism) but in the strength of del Toro's imagery: there is a consistent emphasis on the insect and the clockwork (images that will become recurrent elements throughout all of del Toro's subsequent work) and an interest in the reconfiguration of religious imagery. This is most explicit in the protagonist, Jesus Gris – his name literally translates as Grey Jesus, an apt name for a man who dies and is then resurrected as an immortal vampire. The insectoid and the idea of resurrection are repeatedly fused together, most blatantly when antagonist de la Guardia says 'Christ walks on water, so does a mosquito' and then in subsequent scenes identifies insects as common bloodsuckers and that, on occasion, spiders and ants can resurrect themselves. The presence of such religious imagery can be easily ascribed to del Toro's upbringing and his reaction to religious ideas, constructs and imagery. It could be argued that, although he has described himself as 'a raging atheist', religious imagery still holds a great power for del Toro and through his narratives and his fusing of it with the iconography of the horror film is in fact exploring his personal understanding of such concepts.

Of further interest is that *Cronos* would be the first film that del Toro would work on with cinematograpeher Guillermo Navarro and actors Ron Pearlman and Federico Luppi: since *Cronos* Navarro has been the cinematographer on all but two of del Toro's films (*Mimic*, 1997 and *Blade 2*, 2002) while both actors have repeatedly appeared in subsequent films by del Toro – Pearlman appears in *Blade 2* and both *Hellboy* films (2004, 2008) while Luppi appears in both *The Devil's Backbone* and *Pan's Labyrinth*.

Although *Cronos* was highly successful, it would be another four years before del Toro would direct his next film, *Mimic*:

> **At the end of *Cronos* I was in incredible personal debt to the tune of a quarter of a million dollars; I may have made a career on *Cronos* but I certainly didn't make any money. I was desperate because I was in no position to have this kind of debt... Out of the blue came the offer to meet with Universal Studios to discuss the possibility of a project. On meeting with them it was explained that they would pay me $125,000 for writing a screenplay. (Wood, 2006: 37)**

Believing this would be his next film, del Toro adapted Christopher Fowler's novel *Spanky*[4] but it was rejected by Universal on the grounds that it was both too dark and seemed a confusion of genres as the film began as a comedy but steadily descended into 'tough horror film' (ibid.). Following this setback the chance to direct *Mimic* arose but at this stage it was only going to be one of three shorts that would form an anthology film. Working on the script, del Toro developed it into a feature and the film was put into production.

Although the film offered del Toro his first Hollywood movie it would also be his first experience of the comprises an emerging director has to make on such films. During the production, del Toro and Dimension Films producer Bob Weinstein argued over creative differences, differences that would result in del Toro being temporarily sacked before being re-hired to complete the film. Del Toro has regularly spoken about the difficult experience of directing *Mimic*, stating in one interview that the finished film is 'like having a beautiful daughter whose arms are chopped off' (Anon., n.d.).

Del Toro has often expressed in interviews how unhappy he was with the final film but he also acknowledges the studio's concerns over the budget:

> **Back then [*Mimic*] was the most expensive movie Dimension had ever made and it was also by far the most expensive movie I had ever done. I experienced many hardships with that movie. I sustain the belief that you learn through pain and I certainly learned a hell of a lot... As well as being hard for me, [*Mimic*] was also a hard movie for Miramax to make and I didn't make it any easier on them. At the end of the day with a cold head and a cool heart I see that they wanted to do *Alien* and I wanted to do *Mimic* and so we ended up with *Alien*[3]. (Wood, 2006: 38–9)**

In addition to this, del Toro has also stated that the difficulties and interference of the studio pushed him into learning new techniques and engaging with new equipment, experiences which would directly have an effect on his next film, *The Devil's Backbone*:

> I'm thankful for *Mimic*. I learned a lot about technique and new toys and new camera rigs and simple digital effects and I applied all of that in a much smaller budget of less than six million dollars [on *The Devil's Backbone*]... [The studio] pushed me to try new stuff and I realised I was good at certain things that I never tried. It widened my range of camera moves and storytelling. So you can learn more from a hard experience than a nice one. (Kaufman, n.d.)

References

Anon., n.d. *Mimic*. [Online] Available at: http://en.wikipedia.org/wiki/Mimic_(film) [Accessed 12 March 2009].

Chun, K., n.d. *What is a Ghost? An Interview with Guillermo del Toro*. [Online] Available at: http://www.cineaste.com/what.htm [Accessed 15 October 2008].

del Toro, G., 2004. *Guillermo del Toro Commentary. The Devil's Backbone* [DVD], California: Sony Picture Classics.

del Toro, G., 2006. *Extended Interview with Director Guillermo del Toro. Cronos* [DVD], London: Optimum Home Entertainment.

DePalma, A., 1994. *From a Mexican Grave comes Cronos*. [Online] Available at: http://query.nytimes.com/gst/fullpage.html?res=9804E1D7103DF933A15750C0A962958260&sec=&spon=&pagewanted=all [Accessed 20 February 2008].

Kaufman, A., n.d. *No Mimic: Guillermo del Toro declares his independence with Devil's Backbone* [Online] Available at: http://www.indiewire.com/people/int_delToro_Guiller_011127.html [Accessed 16 October 2008].

Romney, J., 2006. *Guillermo del Toro: The Monster Man.* [Online] Available at: http://www.independent.co.uk/arts-entertainment/films/features/guillermo-del-toro-the-monster-man-424957.html [Accessed 24 March 2009].

Wood, J., 2006. *Talking Movies.* London: Wallflower Press.

Endnotes

1   The UK promotional material for *Hellboy 2: The Golden Army* proudly proclaimed 'From the visionary director of *Pan's Labyrinth*'.

2   Dick Smith (born 26 June 1922, Larchmont, New York) is a renowned make-up artist whose work includes *The Exorcist* (William Friedkin, 1973), *Taxi Driver* (Martin Scorsese, 1976) and *Scanners* (David Cronenberg, 1981). Whilst working as NBC's make-up director, Smith pioneered the use of foam latex prosthetics, applying them in small pieces (as opposed to one overall 'mask') in order to allow the actor to maintain a wide range of facial expressions. This has now become standard practice in film and television make-up. He won an Academy Award for his work on *Amadeus* (Milos Forman, 1984), has had a number of successful protégés (including Rick Baker) and, due to his sustained experimental work in the horror genre, is acknowledged as the father of modern special effects make-up. His website can be accessed at http://www.dicksmithmake-up.com.

3   *Cronos* won nine Ariel de Oro Awards, including Best Picture, Best Director and Best Screenplay for del Toro and was entered into the 1993 Academy Awards as Mexico's entry for Best Foreign Language Film. It also won the Saturn Award for Best Genre Video Release from the Academy of Science Fiction, Fantasy and Horror Films, won the Silver Raven at the 1994 Brussels International Film Festival of Fantasy Film and won the award for Best Direction at the 1995 Fantafestival. *Cronos* was also nominated as one of the best one hundred horror films in the history of film by the British horror magazine *Shivers*.

4   Fowler's novel concerns 23-year-old Martyn who has a dull job, a dull family, very few friends and no girlfriend. All this changes when he meets his personal demon, Spancialosaphus Lacrimosae, whom Martyn befriends. Soon his life changes for the better but these changes come at a price, one that Spanky will extract at any cost.

NARRATIVE

Del Toro has stated that he felt the narrative of *The Devil's Backbone* needed:

> to be constructed on a rhyme. The movie was about a big war but contained inside a small war. If one was a mirror image of the other, the best way to refer to the rest of the movie was by having an opening that was exactly like, or similar to, the ending – but different. And every time one thing repeated itself; it actually enhanced the one before. (Blair, 2001)

There are many instances of doubling within the film: Casares recites poetry twice in the film, Jacinto is injured twice by two different women, two children fall into the cistern water, two children receive an injury to the head, two children sit by the edge of the cistern, two children collect slugs and put them into cardboard boxes, two characters drown in the cistern, the bomb is seen to be dropped onto the school twice, two children hide behind the same pillar at different times, and two characters never get to consummate their love for another. As indicated in this brief list and as will be seen in the next chapter, this sense of narrative repetition constructs parallels and connections between certain characters and so allows for them to be seen and understood from a different perspective.

Perhaps one of the most potent repetitious occurrences in the film is the falling of the bomb: the bomb first falls onto the orphanage during the opening montage and then falls again, in flashback, when Jaime recounts the true events of Santi's murder. The first time the bomb falls it is an act of war, with the Nationalists conducting a bombing run on a Republican dominated area. It is an almost anonymous event, where characters are reduced to one side or the other, to Nationalist or Republican. The second time the bomb drops, this time quite literally in front of Jaime, the event is recoded as something more personal and more horrific: the bomb landing but not exploding is, as del Toro, states 'the hand of God telling [Jaime] "you're a coward"' (ibid.).

On a more complex level, the consistent act of repetition throughout the film suggests that the film itself is uncanny: Freud suggested that one of the most obvious and most frightening occurrences of this sensation was to see the double of one's self or to experience an event twice over, but the second time only slightly differently. Such a quality directly correlates with del Toro's intention that the repeated events in the film are either slightly different (most obviously seen in the sequence concerned with Santi's death) or bringing a new meaning to characters or events. In a way this doubling helps to not only reveal the 'truth' of the narrative events but, as is expected of the uncanny, to heighten the sensation of fear the film generates: the uncanny ghost slowly reveals itself as not to wanting to scare but to avenge their murder, a revelation that displaces the terror from the spectre to the living – it is Jacinto who the characters and audience should be afraid of, not Santi.

While the repetition of scenes and images dominates the film, del Toro integrates two other narrative devices into the otherwise linear narrative of the film: montage and flashback.

Opening Montage

In another instance of repetition, the film is book-ended with an opening and closing montage. A montage is when a series of images – sometimes connected and sometimes not – are edited next to each other to construct a narrative or meaning. The opening montage of *The Devil's Backbone* elides from an image of a doorway to a falling bomb to an injured boy to this boy's body being submerged in water to an image of another boy, his face and hands bloody, sitting by the water's edge. The narrative this sequence suggests is that either the bomb dropping has killed the boy or, somehow, one boy has killed the other and has concealed his murder by submerging the body in water.

The narrative purpose of this opening montage is threefold: it primarily sets the scene for the story – a war is taking place – and that a child has been killed, possibly under suspicious circumstance. It also defines the visual tone, signifiers and themes of the film – the use of amber to signify death; the bomb as another deathly metaphor; the water as a tomb, a sense of entrapment. All of this is enhanced by the voice-over with the narrator asking the question 'What is a ghost?' and providing answers throughout the montage: 'A tragedy condemned to repeat itself time and again? An instant of pain, perhaps? Something dead which is still alive? An emotion suspended in time? Like a blurred photograph, like an insect trapped in amber.' This dialogue reinforces both the use of tone and metaphor and again connects amber to death as well as suggesting this colour can also signify an entrapment in time. The voice also acts as a verbal descriptor to the images: the image of the bomb falling is described within the narration as 'An instant of pain, perhaps?'; while the image of Santi's body sinking in the cistern water is described as 'An emotion suspended in time?'. Here the amber colour of the water is signified as timeless whilst the tragic death of the child is 'held' still in the timelessness of the water.

The voice-over also functions in a more cryptic manner and so foretells events that will take place within the film. This is clearly seen when the image of the kitchen doorway is accompanied by the narrator asking 'What is a ghost?'. The connection here will be discovered in the film when Carlos, in his quest to find out what a ghost is, enters through that doorway and finds the spirit of Santi haunting the vaults of the cistern. It also occurs when the image of Santi's body drops into the water as the voice says 'Something dead which is still alive?'. This, of course, references the fact that although Santi is dead, he will live on as a spectre throughout the narrative.[1]

The closing montage is less narrative-driven and functions more as a series of images which offer a sense of closure. This montage begins with the same image as the opening montage, a medium close-up of the arched doorway to the cistern, cut against an image of Santi standing on the cistern water. A series of cross-dissolves follow: from the wreckage of the orphanage to Jacinto's body floating in the water to Jacinto's photographs floating in the water to the bomb in the courtyard to moving images of the surviving boys leaving the school. The sequence finishes with the ghost of Casares following the boys to the edge of the school gates. The images mark the end of the narrative events in a subdued manner, the calm, as it were, after the storm of Jacinto's rage.

The voice-over narration is similar to the opening montage but concludes with an extra sentence 'A ghost. That is what I am'. This additional line of dialogue indicates that the voice both now and at the start was that of Casares. Given this, and that the montages both open and close the film, it can be suggested that the film is a flashback of sorts, functioning as

Casares' recollection of the events from Carlos' arrival at the school to his departure from it.

Flashback

Susan Hayward describes a flashback as 'a narrative device used in film to go back in time to an earlier moment in a character's life' (1996: 122) which is then (usually) narrated by that character. Because of this, what is seen during the flashback is subjective; it is only their interpretation of events. Hayward continues by stating that flashbacks 'almost always serve to resolve an enigma (a murder...)' and that they 'are by nature investigative or confessional' (ibid.). She also suggests that a flashback is signified to the audience through a close-up of the narrator's face which cross-dissolves to the start of the flashback. This visual transition from present to past is usually supported by the narrator's voice carrying over the image of the present to the image of the past. Such methods are used exactly by del Toro to reveal the truth of Santi's death: having survived Jacinto's first assault, Jaime and Carlos sit together and talk, the conversation eventually turning to Santi's death. Jaime says that 'I saw everything. It started in the cellar'. As he says 'everything' the cross-dissolve begins and the close-up of Jaime's face disappears as an image of the cistern water appears. The flashback narrative then unfolds in an almost linear and subjective manner as all that is seen (apart from the images of Santi sinking) can be ascribed to Jaime's point of view. The sequence concludes with a reversal of the opening cross-dissolve as Jaime touches the fallen but unexploded bomb back to the same close-up that begins the flashback. As Hayward suggests, Jaime's flashback is confessional and solves the murderous riddle that began the film in the opening montage. The importance of this flashback is not necessarily its confessional content but more the fact that Jaime has finally confessed the events to someone so it acts as a cathartic act, a quality made all the more emotional given that he chooses to tell Carlos, the boy he bullied but now calls his friend.

Narrative Context: The Spanish Civil War

In the early 1930s Spain was politically divided. After the fall of Primo de Rivera and the Spanish monarchy in 1930, the dominant political groups were the monarchists and the Falange who stood in opposition to the Republicans, the Catalan and Basque separatists, socialists, communists and anarchists. Within this power struggle lay the origins of the Spanish Civil War. In 1936, the elections handed power to the left-wing Popular Front government, a victory that would cause strike action, rioting and planning of military coups. One of these plots, led by General Jose Sanjurjo and General Francisco Franco, would result in the first decisive attempt to take the power from the Popular Front. Although the initial attack itself was unsuccessful, its repercussions led to the beginning of the civil conflict: Franco's Nationalist army began a full scale attack against the Republicans, first taking the Basque region and then territories between Barcelona and Valencia. The Republicans continued to fight back but soon Barcelona fell and then Madrid. With such territories now under Nationalist control, Franco became the de facto head of the Spanish state and the Falange was made into the sole legal political party of Spain. The Civil War ended after a three-year struggle on 1 April 1939. With the Nationalists in power all right-wing parties were bought together under Franco's regime and so began Franco's dictatorship which would last until his death in 1975.

Both sides gained international recognition during the conflict: the Nationalists received support from the right-wing governments of Italy, Germany and Portugal whilst the Republicans predominately gained the support of the Soviet Union and Mexico as well as receiving aid in the form of the Internal Brigades. Because of the right-wing politics of the Nationalists many citizens from many countries considered the conflict to be one against the ideology of Fascism, an interpretation that has led to the conclusion that the war added to the increasing tensions in the build-up to World War II. Indeed, Italy and Germany provided support for the Nationalists through tank units and ariel bombing campaigns, the Civil War providing an opportunity for the Axis powers to experiment with and to measure the effectiveness of their military machines. Within this civilian conflict friend fought against friends, neighbours against neighbours and family members took up arms against each other, resulting in the deaths not only of active military participants but also civilians as well. Alongside this were the atrocities committed by both sides during the conflict, with women and children being executed alongside those who had differing political or religious beliefs. These assaults became know as the White Terror (the Nationalist atrocities) and the Red Terror (the Republican atrocities). In addition to this, the fight against Fascism also stirred great media interest, particularly in light of the then emergent mass media. As a consequence famous writers such as Ernest Hemmingway and George Orwell documented the war alongside the reportage photographer Robert Capa.

For a film that is set in the final months of this violent and tragic war, there is very little visual evidence of it. This lack of 'war' content was a deliberate strategy on del Toro's part as he chose only to show it twice and have it alluded to during brief moments of dialogue:

> I knew I had to show the war at least once or twice and I decided to show the war in two different terms: one was just this beautiful, distant image of the bomb falling… and then the only other time I wanted to show [it] was through that scene where they are shot in the back of the head. (2004)

Del Toro then defines the war primarily through the unexploded bomb and so turns this weapon into a powerful and potent symbol throughout the film. In many ways the bomb as symbol is passive and does not operate on an emotional level – it signifies violence but does not actually depict the act itself. This is in direct contrast to the other image of the war used by del Toro, the village sequence in which Carlos' tutor Ayala and his friend are executed.

In his Director's Commentary, del Toro suggests that the symbolic nature of the bomb allows it to function as a distant representation of the war (2004) but the execution scene brings it to the foreground of the viewer's attention:

> [I wanted the war to be] individualised to a character [the audience] met in the opening, a character that was injured and now he is being killed so that would hopefully

make the war a little more painful or a little more human to [the audience]. (ibid.)

Del Toro ensures these qualities are felt by filming the scene in tight close-ups: the eye contact between Ayala and Casares is emphasised by this choice of shot as is Ayala's terrified expression. This choice of shot also creates a shallow depth of field and so puts the Nationalist executioner out of focus and so renders him just as a blur, a faceless and violent representation of the side of the conflict. Del Toro adds further emotional emphasis through the editing of the sequence: after Ayala has been forced to turn around, del Toro cuts from execution to Casares back to the execution then back to Casares. Each time the edit returns to Casares, the camera has moved closer to him and so suggests a 'movement' into his fear: the emotions this character feels are literally brought to the fore of the screen and generate greater empathy between audience and character.

On perhaps a more abstract level, the possibility of neighbour fighting neighbour, friend fighting friend and family fighting family during a civil conflict is embodied within Jacinto's relationship to Carmen and Casares: as an orphan, he is in one sense Carmen and Casares' adopted son. These surrogate parents have raised, educated and fed him and the other orphan boys and, by doing so, have formed a family of sorts. When Jacinto begins his attack on the school, his violence can be read not just as an attempt to steal the gold but also as a direct assault on the family unit. The destruction he causes results also in the immediate death of his 'mother' and his orphan 'brothers' as well as the drawn out death of his 'father'.

Such a reading suggests that the violence of the Civil War is literally being played out within the confines of the school, one validated by the political associations del Toro provides his characters with: from the very start it is clear that both Carmen and Casares are Republicans but Jacinto's political leanings are less defined and a little ambiguous. The music he listens to functions as an aural signifier that aligns him with Nationalism while his friends – Marcelo and Pig – are seen talking with the Nationalist soldiers. Perhaps the biggest visual signifier of his political beliefs is his aforementioned attack on the school: the school is a Republican stronghold and those who live within it are either supporters of the Republican cause or the orphaned children of Republican families. With this space being so clearly defined as Republican any attack on it from the outside must be, given the context of the Civil War, by their enemy, the Nationalists. This alone signifies Jacinto's political alignment but it is another question as to whether he actually *understands* that is what he is: while the other adult characters verbally identify their political stance, Jacinto never once mentions politics. Instead his violent actions are motivated purely by greed and his desire for a better life. Such occurrences suggest an ambiguity and so, given this, it is viable to suggest that Jacinto is a proto-Nationalist, meaning that Jacinto is becoming a Nationalist perhaps without realising it.

Jaime's bullying of Carlos and the other boys might also be read as an integral part of this interpretation: Jaime represents a young version of Jacinto in that where Jacinto 'bullies' Carmen and Casares through verbal abuse, Jaime physically bullies Carlos, Gálvez and Owl. The conflict then plays out on both the large and life-threatening scale of the adults and then on the smaller scale of the children. This reduction of adult events and activities down to the level of the children becomes a recurrent motif throughout the film, most notably occurring in Jaime's affections for Conchita and when

Carlos, Gálvez and Owl move a statute of Christ as punishment for going down into the cistern.

The combination of these interpretations suggests then that although del Toro only chooses to show the actual Civil War through the unexploded bomb and the brief scene in the village, he is actually allegorising the war and its devastating consequences constantly throughout the film.

Narrative Location: The Spanish Plain

Surrounding the school is the vast empty space of the Spanish Plain. First seen when Carlos, Ayala and Domìnguez are driving towards the school, this landscape is shown to be a barren and hostile environment. There are no signs of life, be they animal or vegetation, just a seemingly endless expanse of desert, all baking under the heat of the sun. As the film progresses, the isolation of the school within this landscape is verbalised by Carmen and then much later by Conchita, who both suggest the nearest point of civilisation, the village, is at least a days walk away. Such a distance puts further emphasis on the sheer scale of the desert, compounding the sense of isolation the school is within. Although this distance is perceived as a negative, it also contains a contradictorily positive in that the school is so far away from areas of civilisation it is unlikely that the Nationalists will move that far out in an effort to find Republicans. The distance then becomes an empty barrier between those at the school and Civil War, perversely protecting it whilst simultaneously stranding it in the middle of absolutely nowhere.

Narrative: Location – The Village

This location is eluded to a number of times in the film but is only seen once, during the sequence in which Casares witnesses the execution of members of the International Brigade. The primary narrative purpose of the village is to emphasise the distance between the school and this space of civilisation: when Carlos is taken to his bed by Carmen she comments that 'It's a day's walk into town. The nights are cold and the days...'. She pauses here in her dialogue before continuing by saying that '... there are no bars here. This isn't a prison', a comment which only reinforces the sense of entrapment and isolation Carlos and the other boys feel at the school. Much later, after Jacinto has all but destroyed the school, Conchita says to Jaime 'They won't have heard the explosion in town. And it was just one of many. We can't expect any help. If I walk all night I'll get to town by noon tomorrow.' In between these lines of dialogue is Casares and Conchita's trip to the village itself. When Jacinto and the boys load the truck it is mid-morning but by the time Casares and Conchita arrive it is late evening. Civilisation then – or help and protection, given the events that take place later in the film – is a long way off. These visual and verbal signifiers all combine to create the sense of sheer isolation the school exists within: standing in the middle of that nowhere space of the Spanish Plain, the school becomes analogous to the opening dialogue about ghosts for it too can be read as an 'insect' trapped in the amber of the desert.

Very little of the village itself is shown within the film. Only a house or tavern (but even that is out of focus and in the background) and the bombed out wreckage of other buildings are seen. In this evening scene, the village is illuminated by moonlight, a crisp clear light that casts everything in a cold, gun-metal blue[2] creating pockets of deep shadow. Further

30

illumination comes from small fires that create areas of flickering amber light. Whilst suggesting the possibility of warmth they in fact offer only the opposite for the soft light reveals the horror of war as Casares witnesses the execution of the nine Republican soldiers.

The brief presence of the International Brigade lends to the film a certain sense of realism through historical accuracy: the International Brigades was initiated by the French Communist Party Leader Maurice Thorez who called for an international force of volunteers to fight alongside the Republican forces. Joseph Stalin supported this call for armed unity and by 1936 an international recruitment centre was established in Paris alongside a training camp at Albercete, Spain. It has been estimated that 59,000 people, most from left-wing political groups, from over 55 different countries[3] answered Thorez's call, volunteers who would be trained and then deployed throughout the conflict. Their presence was invaluable and their worth proved during the defence of Madrid in November 1936.

In relation to this sense of accuracy, del Toro states in his Director's Commentary that very few people 'even in Spain' knew 'that China was so involved in having troops support the Civil War in '37, '38 and later in '39' (2004). He continues by saying that the scene 'caused a lot of arguments because I had to bring documents that proved Chinamen were involved' (ibid.) in the conflict. Their presence within the film but also brings a wider sense of community to the Republican forces, a quality that will be later evidenced when Jaime unites the boys against Jacinto.

Visually, the scene recalls a painting by Francisco Goya, *The Third of May 1808* (1814)[4]: based on the 'invasion' of Spain by Napoleon's army, Goya's painting depicts the execution of Spanish rebels by soldiers of the French army. Art critic Kenneth Clark has stated that he painting is 'the first great picture which can be called revolutionary in every sense of the word, in style, in subject, and in intention' (Clark, 1968: 130).

The two groups within the painting are depicted as defiantly facing each other: the disorganised line of rebels standing opposite the rigidly organised firing squad. Between them stands a large square lantern, its pale yellow light illuminating the scene – the terrified expressions of the captured Spaniards and the bloodied dead bodies lying at their feet. While the faces of the soldiers cannot be seen, the light reveals the faces of the oppressed rebels, personalising them in order to elicit recognition and sympathy within the viewer; while the oppressors, literally faceless within this image, stand with their backs to the viewer as an anonymous and threatening force.

Given del Toro's *auteurist* trait for Catholic imagery and martyrdom, it is unsurprising that this painting carries with it such religious connotations: the central figure of the painting, the revolutionary wearing the white shirt, stands with his arms raised in a pose that recalls the crucifixion of Christ. Correlating with this reading, this figure's right hand appears to bear an injury, a stigmata-like wound in the palm of his hand. Such an interpretation can potentially provide a different reading of the yellow light, suggesting it has the qualities of transcendence in death but due to the stark brutality this light unveils, all sense of the spiritual is lost.

Visually, this painting and the execution scene are quite similar in that they are both lit by a singular light source, an illumination which throws the horror of the events into chiaroscuro relief; the Nationalist soldiers are seen with their backs to the screen, cropped just into the frame or blurred and so rendering them anonymous, faceless; yet the terror of one of the captured revolutionaries is shown in detail through their facial expression.

The sense of terror that the painting communicates – primarily through the expression of the revolutionary – is reflected in del Toro's comments about his feelings in relation to the scene:

> To me it is truly the scariest scene in the movie on a personal level because the seconds that pass from the moment someone turns you around and it's your turn to be shot in the back... I just can't imagine how incredibly long those seconds are and how an eternity can happen in those moments. (2004)

Narrative Location: The School

The school building[5] is the primary location of the film – all of the characters live there – and it is the site of the narrative's main action. Its primary purpose is as a boarding school but in light of the Civil War its secondary and more covert purpose is to be an orphanage for Republican children. Because of this, the building can be interpreted on a more subtle level as a Republican fortress. As most of the narrative events and actions take place either within the confines of the school or in its playground, very little is actually seen of the building's exterior. When it is seen, it appears as if it were a garrison of sorts with high, windowless walls, turreted corners, and huge wooden doors and its large empty yard space at its centre all suggesting the qualities of a castle. This reading is dormant for the most part of the film, only coming to the fore when Jacinto begins his explosive assault: after the initial explosion, del Toro cuts to an almost silent shot of Jacinto, his back to the camera, looking at the building. Even though he stands in the mid-ground, Jacinto appears to be taller then the building, looming over it. This sense of scale makes the previously strong walls weak, an interpretation compounded by the black plume of smoke pouring out the building itself[6].

If *The Devil's Backbone* is a Gothic text then this genre placement has a dramatic effect on the reading of the school. Its isolation, role as a home and resident spectre all suggest that this building can be interpreted as one of Punter and Byron's key tropes of the Gothic, the Haunted Castle. They suggest that the genre's 'central motif is the castle' (2004: 259) and define it as space that is full of dark, winding corridors in which spectres haunt; that has in its basement a dungeon of sorts in which characters are imprisoned; that it is in some sense an ancestral home; and is one that is full of secrets. They also suggest that:

> **paradoxically [the castle is] a site of domesticity, where ordinary life carries on even while accompanied by the most extraordinary and inexplicable of events. It can be a place of womb-like security, a refuge from the complex exigencies of the outer world...**
> **(Punter and Byron, 2004: 261)**

Their description clearly correlates with the school in *The Devil's Backbone* for it embodies the paradox Punter and Byron describe: during daylight hours it is an ordinary domestic space (as seen in the kitchen and dining spaces as much as in the living spaces of Carmen and Casares and the boy's dormitory) but by night the space is transformed by Santi. Externally the building has the visual qualities of a castle whilst inside it is made up of dark tiled corridors that seem to wind off into the deeper recesses of the building. One such corridor is, of course, where Santi haunts and then chases Carlos. As the narrative progresses, the secrets the building keeps are revealed – it is the hiding place of the stash of Republican gold and also the space in which Carmen and Jacinto conduct their illicit affair.

The building's most Gothic space is the cistern: below ground and accessible only by one flight of cutting stairs, this is the school's dungeon. There, in the water, lies Santi, a prisoner in limbo. It is here that Freud's reflections on the uncanny can be applied. He defined the term through the definitions of *heimlich* (homely) and its opposite, *unheimlich*, that which is unhomely. This difference in terms adequately describes the school for it is both a 'homely' place in which the children live and play and are made to feel safe by their surrogate parents, Carmen and Casares; yet it is simultaneously the uncanny space of the 'unhomely' due to the presence of Santi's ghost. Bennett and Royle's interpretations of the Uncanny also have a value here: in their list of defining qualities of the uncanny they cite the fear of being buried alive (2004: 37). They suggest that this can take various forms, from actually being buried alive to being mistaken for being dead to being confined in a tight and claustrophobic space. The former two qualities relate strongly to Santi's death for he is still alive when Jacinto throws him into the cistern. Santi dies not directly from the injury to his head but from drowning. In this instance Santi is 'buried' alive in the water and transforms the cistern from simply a water supply to an uncanny space, a tomb that functions like Punter and Byron's protective womb for the last mortal remains of Santi.

References

Bennett, A. & Royle, N. (2004). *An Introduction to Literature, Criticism and Theory*, 3rd edn. London: Pearson Education.

Blair, A. (2001). *Interview: Guillermo del Toro*. [Online] Available at: http://www.filmsinreview.com/2001/11/22/interview-guillermo-del-toro/ [Accessed 16 October 2008].

Clark, K. (1968). *Looking at Pictures*. London: Beacon Press.

del Toro, G. (2004). *Guillermo del Toro Commentary. The Devil's Backbone* [DVD]. California: Sony Picture Classics.

Hayward, S. (1996). *Key Concepts in Cinema Studies*. London: Routledge.

Punter, D. & Byron, G. (2004). *The Gothic*. Oxford: Blackwell Publishing.

Endnotes

1   It is interesting to note that the way in which the narration functions within the dialogue is evidenced twice in the sequence – a further example of the film doubling itself.

2   The presence of the gun-metal blue illumination makes a further correlation with *Pan's Labyrinth*: in both films any of the scenes in which the Nationalists appear the illumination is cast in this cold light.

3   This included France, Germany, Poland, Britain, America, Canada, China and Italy.

4   *The Third of May, 1808* by Francisco Goya (Oil on canvas, 266x375cm) is on view at the Museo del Prado, Madrid.

5   A further instance of the director's biography intervening in the film; the design of the classroom is based upon the Jesuit school which del Toro attended as a child.

6   The plume of smoke might be equated with the stream of blood that pours from Santi's head, a connection made all the more stronger by the fact that both 'injuries' were caused by the same person, Jacinto.

CHARACTER OUTLINES

The Three Children

Carlos

The film's protagonist, Carlos is, at the start of the film, unaware that his parents are dead. Unlike the other boys in the school, he has had an education that has encouraged an inquiring, inquisitive and open mind. Upon his arrival at the school he is bullied by Jaime but from the very start he decides to stand up to him and consistently defends himself. While this at first causes greater friction between the two boys, Carlos' act of saving Jaime when he falls into the cistern marks the beginning of their friendship. He also takes the blame for the nocturnal visit to the kitchen to ensure that his friends do not get punished. As the protagonist, a number of Carlos' actions move the narrative forward but his role is really more of the instigator of reconciliation: he encourages Jaime to talk about the night of Santi's murder and so steadily helps this boy change from a bully to a leader whilst his investigations into the spectral occurrences enable Santi to communicate his desire for revenge.

Jaime

The eldest boy at the school, Jaime is first positioned as the school bully. In this role Jaime presents himself as an angry youth, one who gets what he wants by force and who uses this sense of authority to try to control the rumours about the possibility of a ghost within the school. As the narrative unfolds, it is revealed that Jaime is in fact a sensitive boy on the cusp of puberty: he demonstrates his affections for Conchita by giving her both a 'ring' and a 'grain of strength'; he is creative, a quality that is embodied in the sketchbook he constantly draws in; and he is, ultimately, very frightened of Jacinto. When he finally confesses to Carlos that he has witnessed Santi's murder he experiences a catharsis for he is confessing that for all his aggression he is actually a coward. Having unburdened himself, he is able to begin his rite of passage and quickly and effectively brings the boys together through his leadership skills. It is his actions and his desire for a twofold revenge (for Santi and for Conchita) that finally save the boys from Jacinto.

Santi

Very little is known of Santi. His time alive is briefly seen in flashback and succinctly shows his close companionship with Jaime. In death, he is at first afraid of Carlos, hiding behind a pillar when this boy comes down into the cistern to look for him. But as the living boy and dead boy continue to meet they find a common ground in which neither is afraid of the other. Eventually both boys come to understand what is required and, with the help of Jaime, succeed in achieving those goals.

As a ghost, Santi obviously has very strong connections to the uncanny: Freud states that 'many people experience the feeling [of the uncanny] in the highest degree in relation to... spirits and ghosts' (1919: 364). When Carlos first glimpses Santi he is not sure what he has seen; then, later that evening, Carlos hears the disembodied sigh and the shadow of the ghost reaching out to touch the curtain, the wet footprints and the smashed pitcher of water. All of these incidents stimulate Carlos's curiosity and his enquiries lead him, on Gálvez's advice, to question the bomb: asking where Santi is, the bomb 'speaks' in creaks and groans and indicates that Santi is waiting for him in the nearby storeroom. Carlos enters the room and sees Santi, his back turned and breathing heavily, blood seeping from his wound. It is in this moment of seeing Santi properly for the first time that Carlos feels the uncanny nature of Santi's spectral appearance for his breathing becomes laboured, his steps forward tentatively and voice tainted with fear as he tries to speak to the ghost. Santi turns and issues his warning that many of the children will soon die, a portent that terrifies Carlos to the extent that he screams – the clearest reaction to any uncanny event – and runs away.

The Three Adults

Carmen

The Principal of school, Carmen is a strong and dominating woman. Throughout the film, various characters' dialogue refers to her husband, Ricardo, who is briefly seen in a photograph in which he and his wife stand, in happier times, alongside Casares. Although a Republican herself, Carmen has very little positive comments about Ricardo, saying that she left him to fight a war and was killed for the dream of his ideals. She also says that she is the one who is really fighting, for she has been left at the school to protect both the orphaned children and the stash of Republican gold. Although she complains about her situation, Carmen never expresses this to the boys; instead she shows herself to be very maternal, acting as both their teacher and their surrogate mother. Her one weakness is Jacinto, with whom she started a sexual affair with when he was seventeen. It is never explained how she lost her right leg.

Casares

An Argentine by birth, Casares has aligned himself with the Republican cause, acting as the school's science teacher as well as its doctor. He is often shown to be a kindly man, a quality which initiates a relationship and bond between Carlos and himself. Throughout the film he talks of poetry and of revolution but is ultimately passive. In this respect he is finally seen as a weak character: because of his impotency he is unable to directly confess and consummate his love for Carmen; and when Jacinto threatens the safety of Carmen and the children he again does nothing. He tells the boys that he will never leave them and will protect them from Jacinto but he dies before he can do this. But Casares keeps his promise and, in the end, returns from the grave as a spectre and helps the survivors to escape from the locked storeroom. The film ends with Casares announcing to the audience that he, a man of science who did not believe in superstition and ghosts, is himself now a ghost.

Jacinto

An orphan who has returned to the school, Jacinto works there as the caretaker. Like Casares, he is first shown to be a responsible adult with an interest in the welfare of the orphans but the narrative soon reveals that he is far from considerate and caring. Motivated by his disgust at his past, he sleeps with Carmen in an attempt to steal the stash of Republican gold, intending to use it to buy a farm and live the life he thinks he should have. Aside from his sexual relationship with Carmen, Jacinto is also involved in a relationship with Conchita, the school maid. While she clearly shows him affection, Jacinto is often dismissive of her and is, more than likely, simply using her for sex. By the narrative's end Jacinto is exposed as a cruel and ruthless young man who will stop at nothing to get what he believes he deserves. It is this quality that transforms him into the narrative's monster: having got away with the murder of Santi, he kills Conchita because of her lack of loyalty and then kills Carmen, Casares and a number of the orphans when he blows up the school. Although it seems he may get away with these killings as well, he is stopped by Jaime and Carlos who force him into the cistern where he is embraced by the vengeful ghost of Santi.

Character Relationships

From these brief character outlines it is apparent that all of the major characters are, in one way or another, involved in a series of triangular relationships:

- Santi is killed by Jacinto, an act witnessed by Jaime.

- Santi was a close friend of Jaime but chooses to communicate with Carlos. Initially Jaime bullies Carlos but soon becomes his friend, suggesting that Carlos takes Santi's place.

- As friends, Carlos and Jaime join forces to overcome the threat that Jacinto presents as well as avenging the death of Santi.

- Casares cannot physically consummate his love for Carmen who slakes her sexual desires with Jacinto.

- Because of the above there is a conflict between Casares and Jacinto as they battle for Carmen's affections.

It also brings to the fore a Gothic doubling of the characters and a sense of pairing between them:

LIBRARY, UNIVERSITY OF CHESTER

CARLOS	SANTI
Living	Dead
Self	Other
Whole	Fragmented
Solid	Transparent
Living in the Present	Trapped in the Past
Inexperienced	Experienced
Emerging	Submerging

CARLOS	JACINTO
Good	Evil
Living in the Present	Trapped by the Past
Inexperienced	Experienced
Impotent	Virile
Pure	Corrupt
Cultured	Savage
Proto-Republican	Proto-Nationalist

CASARES	JACINTO
Good	Evil
Impotent	Virile
Pure	Corrupt
Cultured	Savage
Republican	Proto-Nationalist

JAIME	JACINTO
Saviour	Killer
Saves Conchita	Kills Conchita
Redeemed	Unredeemed

SANTI	JACINTO
Freed from the past	Trapped by the Past

These two different types of relationship show the complex interplay between the characters, a quality that lends to the narrative both a considerable emotional depth but also its central motivation: the narrative is played out and moved forward by each of the characters either resolving the conflicts of their relationships or coming to terms with them. Such a reading connects with the genre classification of 'childhood drama' and the inherent trope of the Rite of Passage while, perhaps on a more tangential level, suggests an alternative genre framework, that of the 'doomed/fated romance'.

Character Names

Within films across a range of genres, the name of the characters often signifies a personal quality that the character themselves embodies or suggests a connection with the wider themes of the film itself. Del Toro has used this strategy in a number of his others films, most notably in the naming of *Cronos'* protagonist Jesus:

> **The idea was that the film takes place at Christmas time which was when Christ is born. So this specific Christ is born at Christmas time. He dies, he's resurrected on the**

third day, he wears a red cloak, he has stigmata and so on. (2006)[1]

In *Cronos*, then, the narrative trajectory of the protagonist, Jesus, is the aligned with the events in the birth, death and resurrection of Christ: Jesus' birth is when he is bitten by the Cronos device and so killing his human 'life'. After three days he is resurrected from this death as a vampire, wearing a red cloak (both a symbol of Christ and of the vampire) and bleeding, hence the stigmata reference. Given del Toro's upbringing with his devoutly Catholic grandmother, it is hardly surprising that his characters are either direct representations of religious figures or their narrative lives are aligned with such figures.

This referencing of religious values via character names extends into *The Devil's Backbone* through the character of Santi: translated, his name means 'saint'. Definitions of the 'saint' range from 'holy person', 'one eminent for virtue', 'one of the blessed dead'. These values can be read into Santi's character for he is, in terms of his spectral return, a being who is perversely blessed: his unfortunate death has reconfigured him into being capable of warning the other orphans of future events and one who is able to help bring them together as a coherent fighting force. This, combined with the guilt Jaime feels for not intervening in Santi's murder, enable the ghost to be avenged.

Whilst Santi's name clearly signifies the nature of his character, the other central characters are not named to signify personality traits but to make paired connections. As del Toro has himself stated, the characters who are equated with Good throughout the film all have names that begin with the letter 'C' (Carlos, Carmen, Casares and, later, Conchita) whilst the characters who are associated with Evil all have

names that begin with the letter 'J' (Jacinto and Jaime).
Dominating this connection is the aforementioned pairing:
Carlos with Casares and Jaime with Jacinto. In each pair
there is a child and an adult and, through narrative events,
it is implied that each child will mature into the adult they
are paired with: Carlos will become as open-minded and as
accepting as Casares whilst Jaime may become as bitter and
as resentful as Jacinto.

Carlos and Casares

Carlos and Casares' relationship begins with the boy's arrival
at the orphanage: having chased after Anya, Carlos stumbles
and falls to the ground, his suitcase falling open. Casares
walks after him and, crouching down beside him, helps to
pick up his belongings, which include a comic adaptation
of *The Count of Monte Christo*. Casares asks 'Has Edmond
Dantes broken out of prison yet? Has he met Abbott Faria?'
Through his tears Carlos says 'They are digging a tunnel. Do
they manage to escape?' 'I don't know,' replies Casares. 'Why
don't you read on and tell me?' Together, they walk back to
the orphanage. It is in these few moments that Carlos finds
a person he can trust in a new and frightening situation
that he has found himself in: their dialogue suggests their
relationship will be one of student and tutor, one that is
formed upon mutual trust and respect.

The pivotal point of parallel between Carlos and Casares
takes place during the scene in which the two discuss the
collection of vitrines which contain deformed foetuses. Having
had his cheek cut open by Jacinto, Carlos sits with Casares
who cleans the wound. As he does so, Casares asks Carlos
if he has read any more of *The Count of Monte Christo* to
which Carlos replies that he hasn't. There is a pause and

then Carlos asks 'Do you believe in ghosts? I think I saw one here.' Casares responds by gesturing to the various medical objects and diagrams in the room, saying 'as you can see, I am a man of science but Spain is full of superstition'. He walks over to one of the many tables, Carlos following him. As he walks he says that 'Europe is sick with fear now and fear sickens the soul'. On the table are four vitrines, positioned in order of height. Each one is full of an amber liquid and a foetus. Turning one of the vitrines around, Casares shows Carlos the foetus' back – the skin is split open to expose the underdeveloped muscle and spinal column. 'In town,' says Casares, 'they call this the Devil's Backbone. They say lots of things. That this happens to children who shouldn't have been born – "Nobody's children" – but that's a lie. Poverty and disease, that's all it is.' Casares points at the amber liquid: 'The liquid they are in is called "limbo water". In the old days it was made with various spices, cloves and rum.' He takes the lid off the tallest jar and, with a ladle, takes some of the liquid out. 'So this is very, very old rum.' He pours the measure into a small glass. 'I sell it in town and the money keeps the school going.' 'Do they drink it?' asks Carlos. 'They say it helps to cure blindness, kidney aliments and also apparently impotence.' Casares pauses then continues, 'Rubbish but, you know; after 60 men will pay anything just to...' and he raises one of his fingers in a gesture to intimate a growing erection. He smiles at Carlos. 'So, if you're going to believe in ghosts and all that rubbish you should have a sip of this to heal your wound.' He offers Carlos the glass but the boy refuses, 'No, I'm not sure that I saw a ghost. May I go now?' Carlos smiles again. 'Yes, of course.' He waits for Carlos to leave the room and then pauses, looking down into the glass, and then quickly gulps the amber liquid down.

In this scene, Casares initially positions himself as a 'man of science' who does not believe in superstition or the supernatural, a quality that is foregrounded in his role as doctor and his knowledge of medicine. While he himself denies the possibility of the supernatural, he is clearly willing to exploit those that do buy selling them bottles of the amber 'limbo water' as a medicinal cure for the ailments he himself describes to Carlos. The essential contradiction of Casares' character is on display at the end of the scene. When he is sure that Carlos has gone, he himself drinks a measure of the foetal water: whilst he may appear to be a man of science Casares is, in fact, as superstitious as the villagers.

Casares' submission to superstition comes not from a belief in the supposed medicinal powers of the fluid but more so from the desperation of his impotent condition: at night he stands, smartly dressed, at the wall between his room and Carmen's and listens to Carmen and Jacinto making love. These sounds, so close to Casares, function to highlight that he is not able to provide Carmen with her physical needs and desires. By secretly drinking the limbo water Casares not only acknowledges to himself his impotence but is also actively and somewhat desperately trying to find a cure for it. Once cured, he can become what Carmen wants him to be – a kind, sensitive and, as equally importantly, virile man. The shift that Casares undergoes in that simple gesture then is from a rational man of science to desperate man of superstition.

This trajectory, from science to superstition, is paralleled by Carlos' narrative trajectory in relation to his understanding of Santi. Carlos first glimpses Santi standing in the arched doorway of the kitchen and then witnesses his ghostly manifestation at his bedside. These initial appearances instil both fear and curiosity within Carlos to the extent that he begins a quest to understand what he has seen (and fears) by asking Casares about ghosts and the other boys (who have a variety of interpretations of the ghost) as well as speaking to the unexploded bomb embedded in the courtyard. After Jacinto has blown up the orphanage, Jaime tells Carlos the truth about Santi and his death at the hands of Jacinto. Armed with this knowledge, Carlos can now confront the supernatural and challenge it: throughout his pursuit of the ghost Carlos has applied a rational thought process which, in the end, leads him to the conclusion that the ghost is real. Just as Casares confronts the possibility of the supernatural by drinking the limbo water, Carlos confronts the supernatural by telling the ghost he is no longer afraid and that he wants to help.

A further instance of connection between Carlos and Casares occurs in their use of the rifle. As Jacinto confronts Carmen about the Republican gold, Casares approaches them. In his hands he holds the shotgun and tells him to leave or be shot. Jacinto, the ever dominating male, turns and with a wry smile asks 'Will his rifle shoot?' a comment that directly mocks Casares' impotence. The scene concludes with Jacinto leaving the orphanage but without Casares firing the rifle. Later, when the boys have attacked Jacinto in the cistern, it is Carlos – and not, as expected, Jaime – who picks up the rifle. Holding it in a similar manner to Casares, he points the gun at Jacinto but instead of firing it, he says 'Santi' and pushes the man into the water with the barrel of the gun. In both instances both man and boy hold a supremely masculine weapon but do not fire it. Instead they use it as a means to wield power but be controlled enough not to use it. This symbolic use of the weapon also draws a parallel with their shared impotency. Both are impotent through age: Casares through being too old and Carlos too young. Their physical impotency is transferred onto the rifle which remains unfired.

Jaime and Jacinto

The relationship between Jaime and Jacinto is based on aggression. The two are hardly seen together and, when they are, there is a deep animosity between them. This is clearly evident in the scenes in which Jacinto 'orders' Jaime to get the petrol tanks to fuel the truck and then later when Jaime has given Conchita the 'ring'. While this aggression may suggest that the characters are related through a sense of opposition, they are in fact, for the most part of the narrative, almost exactly the same.

The most immediate similarity between Jaime and Jacinto is that they are both orphans who have been bought up by Carmen and Casares. A more complex similarity between the two can be seen in their shared role as school bully: Jacinto bullies, threatens and injures the boys throughout the film as a means of asserting his masculinity. In a similar fashion Jaime bullies and threatens the younger boys as a means to assert his authority over them and to get what he wants from them – usually a toy or a comic. Despite these aggressive actions both Jacinto and Jaime are revealed to be cowards. This is revealed during Jaime's flashback where Jacinto is seen to panic when he kills Santi – instead of getting help, Jacinto is scared and hides the boy's body. Jaime watches this happen and, because he is too afraid of Jacinto, does nothing to intervene to save his friend's life.

As the narrative draws to a close, this sense of similarity gives way to difference: when Jaime explains what he witnessed on the might of Santi's death to Carlos he is verbalising his own cowardice, something that the narcissistic Jacinto would never do. By confessing to Carlos, Jaime not only experiences catharsis but also empowerment as it allows him to understand the error of his ways: whereas Jacinto will always be a violent and greedy man, Jaime decides to change.

Del Toro states that this change positions Jaime as:

> ...the bridge between Jacinto and the [other] kids. [Jaime is] the one with the more complex emotions. That's why he shares even the same initial as Jacinto. He is a bully but instead of never changing, like Jacinto, in the middle of the movie, he reaches out to the other children and saves himself. (*Really Scary*, n.d.)

The film for Jaime at least, becomes not only a Rite of Passage narrative but also a narrative of redemption; an instance in which a young man is able to comes to terms with his feelings of guilt and to accept them into his life. Only then is he able to positively transform.

Strong Women: Carmen and Conchita

Although there are only three women within *The Devil's Backbone*, their quiet and subtle depiction as independent, strong and resourceful characters counters Jacinto's monstrous masculine: of the three women only one, Alma, is a minor character. The maths and reading teacher, Alma is briefly seen in the kitchen and dining room, then later walking down a corridor to fetch clean bed sheets. Her most protracted scene is when she attempts to extinguish the fire caused by Jacinto, only to be killed when the cans of gasoline explode.

The other two women, Carmen and Conchita, play much bigger and more significant roles within the film: as the Principal of the school, Carmen functions as both a matriarch and surrogate mother for the children whilst Conchita is Jacinto's girlfriend. The women are unified by the masculine figure of Jacinto – Conchita is in love with him (but it is a love that is barely reciprocated) whilst Carmen is, simply, having sex with him. From the perspective of the masculine of Jacinto both women are rendered almost as a stereotype: both are fixated upon his virile masculinity and are there to service his sexual desires and, by doing so, amplify Jacinto's beauty whilst indulging his selfish ego. As the film develops, the narrative reveals that these women are not as stereotypical as their initial depiction suggests for the events that Jacinto sets in motion allow the women's strength to emerge and to physically manifest itself, a condition of violence that contrasts sharply with the ineffectual violence of the other masculine representations within the film.

Both of these female characters have a pivotal moment that polarises their relationship with Jacinto and ultimately leads to their acts of violence upon him: for Carmen this polarising moment is when she and Jacinto have made love; as they talk a soft amber light fills the room and suggests that these lovers are, like the insects of the film's opening monologue, trapped in the amber of time. This is potentially a perverse reading for within this couple one is young and the other old. For Carmen, this sexual intimacy is a remembrance of youth, a mode personified by the youthful and virile Jacinto. In this respect Jacinto is transformed from the monstrous masculine into a beautifully perverse connection with the past, a sexual link to something long ago and long forgotten. What makes this union all the more perverse is that Carmen knew Jacinto when he was a child and has watched him grow and mature into a handsome young man. The scene raises the troubling question of when it was she began to desire him, which Jacinto alludes to when he says 'The old man loves you. Always has. Even when your husband was alive. I was 17. They took care of the poetry and I of the flesh.' The antagonism between the characters is palpable and, within its tension, again gives form to the underlying political conflict of the film: with Carmen operating as a signifier of the Republicans, Jacinto fulfils his role as an emerging Nationalist. Del Toro has commented that 'the sexual moment between [them becomes] a moment of power. It's not a pleasurable and liberating moment, it's a mutual mind-fuck and as [such] a crystallisation of internal disruption and the class struggle [within the school]' (Chaw, n.d.). Once again, the impact of Jacinto's past becomes evident, but perversely so for this time he is literally making love to it, arguably in a Freudian sense having sex with his (surrogate) mother which usurps the role of the (surrogate) father, Casares.

Carmen and Jacinto

As the film draws towards its end, the repercussions of this sex scene are felt: having been convinced by Casares that they are in danger from the Nationalists, Carmen makes preparations to leave. Her first act is to open the safe, finally revealing the gold to Jacinto. The subsequent dialogue plays out in a similar manner to the sex scene but this time in terms of a reversal for the two characters:

Jacinto: Are you leaving? Where are you going? What about me? Fuck me, right?

(He turns his back and, whilst looking Conchita directly in the eye, he wipes Jaime's knife on his sleeve and then tucks it into his belt.)

Jacinto: That's good. You can go but the gold stays here.

Carmen: The gold? Is that all you care about?

Jacinto: That's it.

(Carmen slams the safe shut and picks up her walking cane.)

Jacinto: What are you doing?

Carmen: I hid you here so you wouldn't die outside with no one to mourn you.

Jacinto: Give me the key.

Carmen: You know what? Of all the orphans you were the saddest. The lost one. A prince without a kingdom.

Jacinto: Shut up!

Carmen: The only one who was really alone.

Jacinto: I said shut up.

(Their dialogue is interrupted by Casares who, with Conchita, stands behind them, shotgun in hand.)

Casares: Get out of here or I'll shoot you.

Jacinto: Look who's come to save you. The old sage. Will his rifle shoot? You know that while you whisper sweet things to this old hag I'm the one who has to screw her?

(Jacinto turns and Carmen strikes him across the face with her walking cane.)

The opening line of dialogue makes the relationship between this scene and the earlier sex scene apparent: 'Are you leaving? Where are you going? What about me? Fuck me, right?' says Jacinto in what seems like a moment of honest rejection. And this is, ultimately, what it is. Carmen has used Jacinto for sex and now that the situation has become more dangerous, she rejects him. Jacinto's dialogue makes it blatantly clear what they both already knew – he was just being used and in being used he is once again grounded as the abused, the loser and the weakest in the group. Carmen's rejection of him effectively and without violence removes all his potential power as a masculine. He is simply an attractive and virile body, nothing more but the surface of masculinity.

With such feelings now exposed, Jacinto's plan to obtain the gold is all but over, hence the subsequent shots in which he turns his back upon Carmen whilst cleaning the knife. In these brief images, the full predatory nature of Jacinto is seen: del Toro suggests through these images that he will now take the gold by force, probably killing Carmen in the process. The lingering image of the knife being cleaned and then being thrust into the leather belt exaggerates the phallic potential of the weapon, a potency that is also amplified by the previous line of dialogue: 'Fuck me, right?' The knife as virile phallus constructs an ambience of impending sexual violence; that the male penetration of the female will play out again, only this time with weapons, violence and deathly consequence.

As the scene unfolds the reversal of power becomes evident: where Jacinto had taunted Carmen with the truth of their sexual relationship during their sex scene, so Carmen now confronts him with her interpretation: 'I hid you here so you wouldn't die outside with no one to mourn you... Of all the orphans you were the saddest. The lost one. A prince without a kingdom... The only one who was really alone.' As Carmen delivers her dialogue, stern and unblinking, Jacinto interrupts her, repeatedly telling her to 'shut up'. Again, the dialogue and not physical actions, undermines his virility and his masculinity – he is, and always will be, a prince without his kingdom, a little boy lost and alone.

This is one of the most violent scenes in the film, not just because of Carmen's act of striking Jacinto itself, but because of what it expresses. In striking the young man, Carmen vents (or perhaps exorcises) her shame at their relationship. The force of this anger breaks Jacinto's nose and so corrupts the very thing she was initially attracted to – his youthful beauty. Having fallen from the force of the blow, and with blood streaking down his face, Jacinto's very masculinity is broken, fracturing the beauty into a grotesque: hit by the woman he tried to use and abuse, he rests upon the stone floor, humiliated in front of the impotent masculine (Casares), his girlfriend and the boys he bullied.[4]

Conchita and Jacinto

Like Carmen, Conchita's narrative trajectory brings her first
into unity with Jacinto and then steadily draws her away
from him until she encounters him in a pivotal moment that
polarises their relationship. Such an encounter can only
lead to conflict, a situation which will allow her strength
and defiance to manifest itself. For Conchita this pivotal
moment occurs after Carmen has exiled Jacinto: as already
described, this scene is the instance in which Carmen's power
over Jacinto is bought to the fore and used to successfully
ridicule Jacinto and exposes him for what he is – a weak
and vain individual who seeks to steal in order to obtain his
desire. Standing behind Casares during this conflict, Conchita
witnesses this exposure of Jacinto, forcing her to question
their relationship and to instigate the emergence of her own
strength and defiance. As a consequence her pivotal scene
with Jacinto occurs when she discovers him pouring petrol
over the safe: holding the loaded shot gun previously held by
Casares, she approaches him and asks:

Conchita: What are you doing?

(Jacinto smiles at her as he continues to pour the petrol.)

Jacinto: Did you think someone would just give us a
farm? (He looks down at the shot gun.) What
are you doing with that?

(Conchita pulls back the hammer as Jacinto approaches
her.)

Conchita: You're crazy. They are all inside.

Jacinto: You going to shoot me?

(He playfully pushes the gun away. He does it again, a
sadistic grin on his face. He pushes the gun away again and

she fires, the shot hitting his shoulder.)

In this scene Conchita's emergent strength is at first tested and then given vent: Jacinto's dialogue, as it was with Carmen, reveals a certain confessional truth about their relationship in that in his role as provider Jacinto simply does not have the means to provide. His comment 'Did you think someone would just give us a farm?' destroys Conchita's fantasy surrounding their relationship, corrupting it with the reality of Jacinto's weakness and poverty. Unable to gain the money by legitimate means, he intends to steal it. Jacinto implies he is stealing it for them as opposed to simply himself. To steal from those that have protected and employed her does not rest easy with Conchita, a value that is compounded by Jacinto's intention to blow up the safe. She says that he's 'crazy' and, like Carmen before her, undermines his masculinity and his desires by pointing the shotgun at him. Jacinto responds in a typically masculine fashion; believing that Conchita will not shoot him, he dismissively pushes the gun away, tormenting her until she does actually shoot the weapon. Although Conchita's shot misses, she is the only person throughout the film to discharge it, aligning her with the masculine power of the gun and the power such a weapon wields. By taking up arms against her lover and by shooting and injuring him, her emergent strength comes to the fore. With such an attack, the masculine power of Jacinto has once again been undermined, usurped, exposed and injured. As to be expected, such assaults upon this fragile male are not tolerated and Jacinto, fuelled by his anger at this humiliation and of his past, ignites the spilt gasoline and blows up the school. In this singular act he manages to fulfil his desire of tearing the school down and, in doing so, kill his surrogate mother and mortally injury his surrogate father. His revenge then is, like most instances within *The Devil's Backbone*, twofold.

Following the explosion, Conchita, the only able adult left, leaves the orphanage to get help by walking through the desert to the nearest town. As she stumbles down the dirt road, she is confronted by Jacinto, who demands an apology, surrender and compliance. She refuses, but, as with Carmen before her, such demonstrations of defiant strength are not tolerated and Jacinto murders her.

Missing Something

Carlos' and Casares' impotence brings to the fore a wider issue that concerns all of the characters within the film in that each one lacks something essential in their life. This 'something' ultimately prevents each of them from achieving their desires. This is most blatantly embodied within the children for they are orphans and so lack their biological parents. In this state, they have to rely on their surrogate parents – Carmen and Casares – to house, feed and educate them. In their innocence, the children trust the adults but, as del Toro himself states, this is misplaced, for:

> ... every character in the movie lacks something. There are no complete characters. Casares is in love but is impotent. He doesn't have the guts to tell Carmen. Carmen is a powerful beautiful, vital, incredible woman but she is anchored in this building by [her missing] leg. She cannot run away symbolically or practically... Jacinto is the perfect sexual lover but he lacks a heart. (2004)

This quality of lacking motivates each of the adult character's actions as they attempt to obtain or achieve in order to become complete: this is clearly seen in Casares who resignedly puts his faith in the limbo water to restore his potency and in Jacinto who is attempting to steal the

Republican gold in order to finance his future. Their attempts to become whole lead only to further failure, regret and, ultimately, violence. In this moment, all that is and all that could have been is destroyed, leaving all of the adults dead and the children with nothing: without their surrogate parents and their home destroyed, the boys have nothing left but the weapons they fashioned to attack Jacinto with. Alone, they walk out into the Spanish Plain to confront whatever lies ahead.

While the drive to become whole motivates each of the characters, their very lacking is in contrast to the structure of the narrative: as will be described later, the narrative both repeats, mirrors and doubles itself throughout the duration of the film. This quality lends the narrative a sense of unity and wholeness, something which the adult characters themselves do not have. Instead they all remain asymmetric: Carmen is lopsided because she is missing a leg, Casares isn't a 'real man' because he is impotent, and, finally, Jacinto destroys his childhood so he is a man without a past.

The Failure of the Adult

By the end of the film it becomes apparent that all of the adult characters – Carmen, Casares, Jacinto and Conchita – have, in one or another, let the orphans down. Del Toro has commented that the narrative's end has:

> ...the kids coming together as one, once every single adult has let them down. Every single adult is disappointing, as they often are in childhood. They promise you things they don't deliver; they theorise about things they don't act upon; and all of them seem incomplete characters. (Blair, 2001)

Perhaps the adult that seems to fail the most is Casares for he is clearly incapable of taking action: aligned with the Republicans, Casares enjoys talking about the rhetoric of revolution and freedom, of learning and quoting poetry that expresses similar sentiments; yet when Jacinto's actions turn violent and those he cares for begin to die he is still unable to act. In del Toro's words he is a 'completely impotent character beyond the sexual aspects [of his impotency] – he is politically impotent, philosophically impotent'. He concludes by saying that 'he is ultimately a revolutionary man that is incapable of firing a shot. A revolution, now and then, requires a shot' (ibid.).

While del Toro's observations on this character are true in his physical life, they do not fully equate with Casares' afterlife: having died while waiting for Jacinto to return, Casares continues to protect the boys in death. In an ironic twist, Casares, the man who told Carlos that ghosts did not exist, returns as one to help the boys escape from the locked store room. This singular action of freeing the boys enables them to put into action Jaime's plan to overthrow the fascistic Jacinto: it would seem that for Casares, one can only become potent politically in death and that one's political beliefs and actions can continue to reverberate and impact upon the living whilst in this state.

References

Blair, A. (2001). *Interview: Guillermo del Toro.* [Online] Available at: http://www.filmsinreview.com/2001/11/22/interview-guillermo-del-toro/ [Accessed 16 October 2008].

Brinks, E. (2004). 'Nobody's Children: Gothic Representation and Traumatic History in *The Devil's Backbone', Journal of*

Composition Theory, 24 (3), pp. 291–312.

Chaw, W. (n.d.). *Speak of 'The Devil's Backbone'*. [Online]
Available at: http://www.filmfreakcentral.net/notes/
speakofthedevilsbackbone.htm [Accessed 16 October 2008].

del Toro, G. (2004). *Guillermo del Toro Commentary. The Devil's
Backbone* [DVD]. California: Sony Picture Classics.

del Toro, G. (2006). *Extended Interview with Director
Guillermo del Toro. Cronos* [DVD]. London: Optimum Home
Entertainment.

Freud, S. (1919). *The Uncanny*. In: A. Richards & A. Dickson,
eds., 1991. *Penguin Freud Library*. London: Penguin.

Hurley, K. *British Gothic Fiction, 1885–1930*. In: Hogle,
Jerrold E. (ed.), *The Cambridge Companion to Gothic Fiction*.
Cambridge: Cambridge University Press, 2002. [Q: YEAR?]

Punter, D. & Byron, G. (2004). *The Gothic*. Oxford: Blackwell.

Really Scary, n.d. *Guillermo del Toro shows Really Scary The
Devil's Backbone*. [Online] Available at: http://www.reallyscary.
com/interviewdeltoro.asp [Accessed 16 October 2008].

Endnotes

1   A connection between Jesus and Casares can be made in light of del Toro's religious
     interpretation: not only are both characters played by the same actor – Fred Luppi – but
     they both have a similar narrative trajectory: as del Toro has commented in interview,
     Casares 'dies a martyr's death and returns from the grave to guide his diminutive
     acolytes to salvation' (Chaw, n.d.).

2   As will be described in detail later, the cistern can be read as a psychological space,
     one which Jacinto protects because of the crime he committed in there. In this scene,
     a similar reading can be generated as the cistern is also the space in which Jaime was
     unable to overcome his cowardice. As a consequence he, like Jacinto, wants to protect
     and conceal the space from the other children and adults.

3   Davies' observation that only Jacinto is seen wearing a singlet is not strictly true – Pig,
     the large, fat man who helps Jacinto is also seen wearing a singlet that reveals his
     sweaty body and layers of fat. Arguably, this in itself works in Jacinto's favour for it

serves to highlight his muscular and toned body.

4   Carmen's power at usurping the masculine is twofold in this scene: she not only humiliates Jacinto she also, inadvertently, humiliates Casares. Holding the shot gun before him (or more precisely, resting it near his groin as a possible potent phallic substitute), Casares has the potential to emerge as a strong (but impotent) masculine. Holding the gun and threatening Jacinto is an act of masculine/patriarchal protection, an act made all the more evident by the presence of the 'weak' maid and the young boys positioned behind him. Yet this moment, what could have been Casares prime defining moment of masculinity, is quickly undermined by Carmen. Her striking of Jacinto exorcises her shame at her relationship with him but also clearly and quite succinctly demonstrates that she does not need a male to protect her from danger. Having struck Jacinto, she moves forward, standing over him. As he simpers in pain, she stands ready to strike again, if need be. As a consequence, the orphanage as a matriarchal space is made physically evident.

ELEMENTS, THEMES AND MOTIFS

Amber

In terms of lighting the film is dominated by a strong amber tone. While dietetically this light comes from the sun beating down on the plain and the school, the light also has meaning invested in it: the opening montage's narration suggests that a ghost, something which is dead but also uncannily alive, is similar to an insect trapped in amber. This suggests that the ghost is a life trapped within a specific moment, locked forever in a singular pose and action. This can be easily applied to Santi for his mortal body is literally frozen in the dirty amber water of his grave, the cistern, whilst in his spectral form his spirit body is held 'frozen' in the ghostly swirl of water that surrounds him.

It is worth noting that throughout the film a number of the key spaces have an oval, almost womb-like form and are predominately illuminated by amber light. This is most blatantly seen in the early appearances of Santi, standing as he does in the arched doorways of the kitchen entrance and the entrance to the cistern stairwell, his semi-transparent form all but a silhouette against the burning amber light.

The analogy of the insect trapped in amber can by extended to the school itself: built in the vast expanse of the Spanish Plain and subject to the searing heat of the sun, the building itself can also be read as an 'insect' trapped in the amber of the desert and sunlight. This reading suggests that everyone – the strong and the weak, the innocent and the guilty, the living and the dead – are all trapped and 'frozen' in time. The desert location reinforces this reading for it is a space seemingly without limits, isolated and timeless.

The meaning of the amber as a signifier of the deathly is also evident in the scene in which Carmen and Jacinto make love: this scene glows with a deep amber light, filling the room with a sense of frozen time but, because the amber colour is connected with death through the opening monologue, the presence of the colour here signifies that the sex taking place is itself 'dead': there is no real love between Jacinto and Carmen nor is there even the pretence of romance or intention of conceiving a child. It is just an act to slake their carnal desires.

Sound

Since the learning experience of *Mimic*, del Toro has become increasingly interested in how sound can amplify both the physical viewing experience of his films and the visual qualities of characters' experiences within the narrative. Within the former, when *The Devil's Backbone* is viewed with surround sound, the environment on the screen is made physical through the sound, so when one of the children runs around the yard the sound of their feet *crunching* on the soil moves from corner to corner of the cinema, a movement of sound that positions the audience within the frame. A further example would be when Santi appears at the end of the corridor to chase Carlos: the sounds he makes are projected from the rear speakers whilst the sounds Carlos makes are projected from the front speakers. This has the effect, as before, of positioning the audience in the middle, with Carlos standing in front of them and Santi behind them.

Santi also offers a prime example of del Toro using sound to exaggerate the visual and physical qualities of the characters. Del Toro wanted Santi's manifestations to have a signature sound cue so he came up with the idea of mixing Coca-Cola with rock salt. This created a strong fizzing sound which was recorded and then digitally processed to make it sound more ethereal. The 'ghostly' nature of Santi's 'sounds' continues with his voice which is made up of three layers: there is the consistent heavy, almost asthmatic, breathing (del Toro again made this sound himself), the child's voice and the soft sound of water dripping. Whenever Santi uses a consonant the sound of water dripping has been digitally added to it. Although this is a subtle use of sound, when the three layers are combined the ghost's voice sounds both spectral – transparent and shifting – and as if it were a liquid – wet and dripping – all of which consolidate Santi's entrapment within the spectral haze of water.

A further instance of altered sound occurs after the secondary explosion: realising that Carmen is still in the school, Casares attempts to rescue her but there is a second explosion, the force of which throws him into the air. When he lands del Toro cuts to a close-up of Casares' face, cut open and bloody from the flying debris. On this cut from explosion to close-up the sound abruptly changes as the force of the explosion has deafened Casares so changing the diegetic sound into a muffled 'internal' diegetic. In this 'internal' sound, everything is dampened down and has a certain liquid quality to it. It sounds almost as if Casares is underwater, an aural quality that tangentially equates him with Santi. In this instance the sound puts the audience into Casares' 'head', a quality del Toro amplifies by then cutting from the close-up of Casares to his point of view: the viewer watches, as Casares watches, the school truck explode, the dramatic sound of this reduced to nothing but a dull, soft thud.

Waiting

The sense of entrapment that pervades the film can provide an alternative interpretation to the reading that the primary characters are all seemingly frozen in time: they are in fact trapped in a repetitious cycle, a repetition in which each character is waiting for something to happen in order to free them:

- Casares is patiently waiting for Carmen to reciprocate the love he has for her.

- Jacinto patiently bides his time as he works his way through the mass of Carmen's keys in order to find the one that will open the school safe.

- Carmen and Casares, along with Jacinto, Conchita and Alma, are all hiding in the orphanage where they are waiting out the Civil War.

- Santi is waiting for the right boy to communicate with and use them to orchestrate his revenge.

- Like Casares, Conchita is waiting for her lover, Jacinto, to fully reciprocate her love as much as she waits for him to gain the finances to fund their dream of buying a farm.

- The bomb in the courtyard continues to tick, waiting to explode.

- Those orphans who are in denial of their parents' death await their return.

For each of the above characters, a personally specific event will break this seemingly endless waiting and will, to a great extent, not only bring them happiness but also, they believe, a new sense of life: Carmen will love Casares, Jacinto and Conchita will have the money to buy their farm and begin a new life, and the children will be reunited with their parents. With such emotionally charged qualities attached to this sense of waiting it is perhaps unsurprising that each desire will come about but in an unexpected and tragic way: the cycle of waiting is broken by Jacinto. Unwilling to wait to steal the gold any longer, Jacinto takes it by force, the explosion that he causes not only destroying the orphanage but also the 'amber bubble' of time. Once destroyed, the wait for each character's desire is over – Casares finally verbalises his love for Carmen, Jacinto finally gets the gold and Santi finally gets his revenge. But while each of the living characters gets what they desire, they are also quickly robbed of it – Carmen dies before being able to reciprocate Casares' affections and Jacinto drowns in a deathly embrace with Santi.

The only primary character who is not overtly waiting is Carlos. As a newcomer to the orphanage, he is not yet integrated into the building's timeless cycle. Instead, he stands on the edge of it, observing all that goes on as he steadily uncovers its secrets. It is his investigation into the ghost of Santi that contributes to the breaking of the cycle. By understanding who Santi is and what he wants, Carlos is able to help Jaime confess his own guilt over his inability to help Santi and come to terms with it, an action that transforms this boy from bully to leader. With this knowledge Carlos is then able to confront the ghost without fear and discover its needs, an understanding which brings about the end of Santi's cycle of waiting for revenge.

Weight

The concept of weight is at the heart of the film's opening and closing events – the death of Santi and the death of Jacinto: as indicated during the opening montage and Jaime's flashback to that event, Jacinto panics and ties Santi's convulsing body with ropes and weights before pushing him into the cistern. Here the attached weights serve as a means to conceal, to drag Santi's body to the bottom of the cistern and to anchor it there, hiding it forever. Later, as the film draws to an end, Jacinto is pushed into the cistern and he too is weighed down, inadvertently, by the gold ingots in his pockets and those tied to his waist. In this instance the meaning of the gold Jacinto so desperately craved is inverted. What he stole in order to give him a new life has only bought him to his death. It would seem then, within the narrative of *The Devil's Backbone*, that the unwillingness to work for one's goals, to be motivated by greed and to steal and then murder is punishable only with death – a cruel appropriate one at that[1].

Throughout the film the Republican gold does not bring anyone wealth, only death. Carmen makes a comment to Ayala that she cannot sell the gold so whilst the school is rich with these ingots, they do not have enough money to buy bread to feed the orphans. Jacinto wants to steal the gold so that he can buy the school and tear it down and then begin a new life elsewhere. For him, the gold will not only facilitate his dream of being rich but will also erase his past, indicating that he believes money can solve all his problems. It would also seem that the gold has a quality of being cursed for all those who come into contact with the gold die: Carmen is seen in the film's early scenes handling the gold and giving some of it to Ayala and his friend, both of whom are later executed by the Nationalists. The building which houses the gold is destroyed, killing Casares and a number of the orphans. Carmen is also killed in this explosion, her connection with the cursed gold made explicit when it is revealed that she has been 'wearing' the gold as she had hidden it, from Jacinto, inside her false leg. As she walks through the dormitories she complains of how heavy her false leg is, so making explicit the connection between the gold and weight. It also makes explicit that the gold is both a mental and physical burden upon her. And there's Jacinto, his sole desire causes his untimely death: with the gold in his pockets and tied to his belt, he is weighted down when he is pushed into the cistern by Carlos. Unable to release these 'weights' of gold, he drowns. Jacinto's 'wearing' of the gold at the moment of his death makes a further, if subtle, connection between Carmen and himself for both 'wear' the gold when they die, both bound down by its 'weight'.

Weight is also briefly mentioned by Gálvez: as punishment for going down into the cistern, this boy along with Carlos and Owl are asked to move a number of religious icons from the storeroom into the yard. One of these is a life-size carving of Christ on the cross. The boys pull off the dusty sheet and, one at each end, carry the icon outside and, with considerable effort, manage to prop it up against one of the walls. Del Toro cuts to a medium close-up of Christ's face, his head resting in the crook of his collar bone, his eyes worn and forehead bleeding. The camera lingers, making a brief connection to Santi: one is a saintly by nature, the other by translation of their name and both have received bloody injuries to the head. Gálvez looks up at him and comments 'Shit, for a dead guy he sure weighs a lot!'

This line of dialogue can be read in two ways: the first and most obvious reading would be to interpret it as the weight of sins, to be burdened with their weight and consequently punished for them. Whilst Christ took on the sins of others, it is possible that del Toro is referring here to Jacinto. This is not to suggest that Jacinto is a Christ-like figure. On the contrary, the parallel relates more to his accidental murder of Santi. Choosing not to get help and then concealing the body is a dreadful sin, one for which he is eventually punished for.

A secondary reading suggests that making the boys carry a heavy replica of Christ on their shoulders is a seemingly appropriate punishment: Christ died for our sins, punished by carrying his cross upon his shoulders to Golgotha. In this brief scene, the punishment is the same but the sin reduced to simply entering into an out of bounds space. It is another instance of reduction, where the script and actions once again scale down adult events to the level of the children.

Entrapment

Near the start of the film, one of the narrative's overarching themes is clearly identified by Carmen: when she shows Carlos to the dormitory, he asks why there are so many empty beds. She replies, 'Some boys run away but I wouldn't advise it. It's a day's walk into town. The nights are cold and the days...there are no bars here. This isn't a prison.'

While her answer tries to diminish the orphanage's prison-like attributes, for virtually all of the main characters, it is precisely that. Prior to this scene, the theme is subtly pre-empted in the brief dialogue between Casares and Carlos when they gather up his belongings:

Casares: *The Count of Monte Christo.* Has Edmond Dantes broken out of prison yet? Has he met Abbott Faria?

Carlos: They are digging a tunnel. Do they manage to escape?

Casares: I don't know. Why don't you read on and tell me?

This dialogue immediately raises the possibility of escape as, at least, questionable – although the characters in the novel are digging a tunnel to escape it is clear that they may not escape at all. An alternative reading of this dialogue would be to suggest that it sets out the basic narrative arc of the film in that a group of boys are trapped in the school and must, somehow escape, and whether they do or not is the excitement and emotional centre of the film:

- The opening narration's description of a ghost places great emphasis on being trapped – 'like an insect trapped in amber' and 'an emotion suspended in time' and 'a tragedy condemned to repeat itself time and again' all suggest that even in death the children and adults of this space will remain trapped in time and space, doomed to forever repeat the moment of their deaths.

- As previously discussed, the school itself is trapped in the middle of nowhere, stranded in the vast expanse of the Spanish Plain. This sense of isolation is clearly defined in Carmen's dialogue – the nearest town is a day's walk across the searing desert.

- As both a physical body and as an ethereal spirit, Santi is trapped within the womb of the cistern and the confines of the school building. It is worth noting that Santi never leaves the confines of the building, even after he has killed Jacinto: it is assumed that once Santi had slaked his desire for revenge then his spirit would be released from limbo but, as the closing montage reveals, his spirit remains forever trapped within the school.

- Santi's entrapment relates, as previously suggested, to the deformed foetuses contained with their glass vitrine wombs in Casares' classroom.

- Carmen is trapped within the school for a number of reasons: she remains there to look after the boys because, as she intimates to Jacinto, no one else will. This emotional attachment extends into her relationship with her husband, who, it is implied, founded the school with her. On a more physical level, Carmen's missing leg seemingly makes it impossible for her to leave the school.

- Because of the above and his love for her, Casares will not leave the school unless Carmen does, regardless of the many times Carmen tells him to leave.

- On a more psychological level, Jacinto is trapped by his past. He believes his childhood was taken away form him because he was an orphan and that such an experience marks him out as both 'different' and unable to cope. For the entirety of the film, he is trying to escape this psychological prison he has constructed for himself, hence the sex he has with Carmen can be considered almost abusive whilst his attempts to steal the gold will allow him to buy the school and tear it down. To escape then, Jacinto must become wealthy and destroy the people and the one building that weigh him down to his past. It is ironic then that he does achieve this, but only in his own death.

- On a lesser level, there are two occurrences of the children being locked in rooms. The first is when Carlos locks himself inside the laundry cupboard to hide from Santi and the second is when Jacinto, Marcelo and Pig lock the surviving children in the storeroom. In both instances, the children are released from the rooms by one of the teachers – Alma and Casares respectively – unlocking the door.

With all of these various permeations of entrapment, the essence of the narrative becomes, as Casares and Carlos discuss in their dialogue, about the attempt to escape. By the end, though, very few have escaped – only the surviving boys are seen to actually leave the building and walk out into the Plain. The others are all dead, with either their mortal bodies buried beneath the rubble or deep within the waters of the cistern, their spirits forever trapped in the limbo of the school.

The Bomb

The bomb appears as the second shot in the film: during the opening montage, a set of bomb doors are seen to open and a single bomb released[2]. This bomb falls into the school yard but does not, for some unexplained reason, explode.

Ellen Brinks connects this event with the narrative's Gothic heritage by suggesting a connection with what is considered to be the first Gothic novel, *The Castle of Otranto* (Horace Walpole, 1759): in her reading of the opening montage, Brinks suggests that the cut between the falling bomb to the image of the mortally injured Santi directly correlates with the opening of Walpole's novel in which the son of the antagonist 'is crushed to death by a giant helmet crashing through the castle's roof' (2004: 262). Brinks interprets the falling helmet as a message 'that the younger generation will be destroyed... by legitimate or illegitimate patriarchal politics' (ibid.). What Brinks is suggesting is that the children of the narrative will be 'killed' (either physically or emotionally) as a result of the actions of their fathers. 'Father' can be interpreted in two ways: as either the parental father who controls the family and the household or the father of a country as personified by the government. These two differing senses of the father have an impact on the children of *The Devil's Backbone*: the parental fathers have made the decision to fight against the Nationalists and have been killed so leaving the boys of the film without parents, effectively 'killimg' their family and their childhood. This is most clearly seen in Jacinto and then later with the boys who survive Jacinto's assault on the school. All of them have had their childhood taken away from them by violence. As the narrative unfolds these boys are again subjected to the patriarchal conflict between Casares and Jacinto. Unable to stand up to Jacinto, Casares unwittingly brings about the destruction of the school and the deaths of a number of the children – again the actions of the father and the dominating masculine figure bring about the literal destruction of the younger generation.

The film's concluding image – of the surviving boys walking out of the ruins of the school and into the bright sunlight – suggests that they are free of such dominating masculine forces; but this ending is ultimately ambiguous, for the boys must now fend for themselves against a much bigger, much stronger and much more violent patriarchy, that of the Nationalist government. Three years on from the events at the Santa Lucia school, it is revealed in *Pan's Labyrinth* that the leader of this group does not escape the violence of this 'father'. Instead his life is absorbed by it and ended by it: in the aftermath of one of the brutal attacks on the Republicans, Captain Vidal of the Nationalist army is seen walking through the corpses, looking for survivors to torture. Amongst them he finds a young man, alive but his throat shot open. Vidal smiles and aims his pistol at this man who, in a futile attempt to save his life, tries to push the gun away. Vidal's grin widens as he toys with the man and then, bored, simply executes him. The camera pans down to the body. The young man is Jaime and lying at his side, also dead, is Carlos. In *The Devil's Backbone* then Jaime and Carlos are able to overcome the singular Nationalist threat of Jacinto but in *Pan's Labyrinth* they are not able to overcome Captain Vidal and his army of Nationalist soldiers. Instead, they stand (as they did when they were children) side by side, using unity and solidarity as a means by which to fight that which oppresses and threatens them. But in this national conflict that is not enough and they die together, as soldiers, as Republicans and as friends.

Given the bomb's placement in the centre of the school yard, it is unsurprising that it functions on different levels for the various characters. But, for all of the characters, the bomb clearly represents the Civil War raging far from the school. Del Toro has commented that he:

> **wanted to have a symbol in the movie that represented war because the orphanage is so far away. I needed something that was almost like a totem that reminded you that you may be far away geographically, but here I am, I'm War. (Really Scary, n.d.)**

The bomb's sole purpose, then, is to destroy and for this one bomb its chance dropping is to destroy the orphanage. But it doesn't. Instead the violent and destructive potential will be neutered in this weapon and instead transferred onto one of the living, Jacinto.

Of all the characters that are in some way connected to the bomb, it is Jacinto who is the most closely connected to it symbolically. Near the beginning of the film, when he talks briefly of his past to Conchita he says that when he was a child he prayed that he could 'tear' the school down. As the narrative unfolds, it becomes apparent that Jacinto is a devious, abusive and violent man, one who is steadily being wound up, frustrated and angered by those around him. He is, in effect, a ticking bomb waiting to explode. And, indeed, in the end, it is Jacinto whose actions cause the destruction, fragmentation and deaths of many of the characters.

Within the political constructs of the film, the relationship between Jacinto and the bomb is clear, for the bomb was dropped from a Nationalist plane and, by the narrative's end, it is clear that Jacinto has too aligned himself with the Nationalists. Within this sense of unity between the man and the object, Jacinto's explosive act physically plays out the Civil War within the confines of the school. His selfish acts bring about the death of the orphaned boys of deceased Republicans and their adult sympathiser/surrogate parents. The explosion functions as a dreadful revenge, a further punishment for the deceased Republicans for not only have they been killed in the act of defending their values and their country, their offspring have also been killed; lest they themselves take up arms. This then suggests a sort of paranoid genocide in that in order for the New Spain to be pure then all traces of its Republican past – be that children or buildings – must be destroyed and obliterated from history.

In her critique of the film, Ann Davies suggests the bomb is also a phallic symbol, but one that ultimately lacks potency:

...yet for all the hugeness of the bomb as phallic symbol this is a bomb that fails to explode. Even during the

cataclysm of the fire and the subsequent explosions caused by Jacinto, in which Carmen, the housekeeper and some of the boys die (with Casares later to die of his injuries), the bomb remains unusually dormant, apparently untouched by the explosive forces raging all around it. (2006: 138)

Although the bomb is impotent, a quality that Alma makes clear at the start of the film when she tells Ayala that it has been diffused, Jaime still believes that it remains active. When walking across the yard to collect water with Carlos, he pauses by it and says:

They say it's switched off but I don't believe it. Put your ear against it, you'll hear it ticking. [The metal 'clunks' as it contracts in the cold night.] That's its heart. It's still alive and it knows we are here.

Jaime's animism of the bomb comes not from his belief that it is physically alive but from the personally symbolic nature of this uncanny object: having witnessed Santi's murder, he runs out of the cistern and into the yard, the bomb drops out of the sky and embeds itself in the earth a few yards away from him. Seeing Santi murdered and then almost immediately seeing the bomb fall but not detonate irreversibly connects that deathly event to that deathly object for Jaime. For him and for him alone, the unexploded bomb becomes both a symbol of his powerlessness to intervene in Santi's death and his cowardice. Unable to reconcile these feelings of failure and fear, Jaime invests the bomb with animistic qualities – the symbolic bomb remains alive for him because the feelings associated with it remain live and unresolved.

While this provides a surface reading of the uncanny nature of the bomb, a re-reading of Jaime's dialogue provides another layer of the bomb's uncanny potential: with the bomb being inextricably linked to Santi, it can be argued that for Jaime the bomb represents the undead Santi: privately Jaime knows that Santi haunts the school's corridors but he repeatedly denies his spectral existence to the others in a further attempt to repress his guilty conscience. In this respect, Jaime's dialogue configures the bomb as a symbolic representation of Santi's ghost: his suggestion that the bomb is dead but alive clearly describes Santi in his spectral state whilst the belief that the bomb is still ticking and so counting down the days to its detonation, correlates with Santi's unresolved connections with the living – whereas the bomb waits to explode and kill, Santi waits for the right child to communicate with in order to orchestrate his murderous revenge.

It is worth noting that del Toro also makes a conscious effort to visually connect the bomb with Santi: apart from the obvious implications of the opening montage which implies the bomb lands, explodes and injures Santi, there is a brief scene near the beginning when Carlos first sees Santi. Having touched the bomb, he turns and sees the boy in the arched doorway to the kitchen. Distracted by the squawk of one of the chickens, he turns and looks back to see the boy has gone. Del Toro then cuts to a reverse shot, using the arched doorway to frame Carlos, the bomb and the dull ochre yard. This singular image makes the visual connection between Santi and Carlos, Santi and the bomb by putting them within the arched frame. This, of course, is another instance of del Toro foregrounding the opening monologue as the image implies that the bomb and Carlos are like 'insects trapped in amber'.

This reading suggests that both Carlos and the bomb are held or trapped in time. Whilst this may be questionable for Carlos, it is not for the bomb: for the adults the only threat it presents is a symbolic one for it has been diffused but for the orphans it is alive and has the potential to explode. Either way, the bomb is held in a seemingly endless stasis – it is immovable according to Alma so will forever remain within the school grounds yet the creaking and ticking 'heart' the boys claim they can hear suggests that it will, at some unexpected juncture, explode.

By the narrative's end there have been two big explosions but neither is the bomb in the grounds. The one thing that should have exploded remains intact. Del Toro has commented on this by stating that:

> I wanted very much to have a symbol that didn't pay off like in a Hollywood movie that is, that exploded at the end. I actually very purposely decided that there was a huge explosion but the bomb remained undetonated. And the reason for this is found in the inaction of objects, because the only way I can deal with war in this movie is to say 'And the bomb is still unexploded in the middle of the patio'. And that's one of the last images in the epilogue, the bomb still there standing proud in the middle of the courtyard. (Really Scary, n.d.)

The Cistern

After seeing the spectre of Santi for a second time, Carlos asks Casares if there are such things as ghosts. As discussed earlier, he answers by stating that he is a man of science and that such things are nothing more than the product of superstition. To prove his point, Casares shows Carlos a series of vitrines. Each one is filled with what Casares calls 'limbo water', an amber mix of rum and spices, which holds in suspension the foetus of a deformed child: their underdeveloped bodies fold in upon themselves, their faces tucked into their chests, their spines twisted and broken. The analogy is not difficult to draw: the vitrines, filled with amber liquid that is flecked with motes of spices, are no different to the cistern and its ochre water that is flecked with dirt and filth. The deformed foetuses, unborn and never aging in the limbo water are no different to Santi who is himself held in an ageless, spectral limbo. If the unborn float within these spaces, then the vitrines and the cistern must be analogies for the space that Freud defined as the most uncanny of them all, the womb.

In death, Santi's mortal body remains protected within the womb of the cistern but as a ghost he is able – in some spectral sense – to be both within it and out of it. Whenever he manifests, Santi appears in a swirl of the cistern's water; a soft smear surrounds him, its gentle swell holds within it the flecks of dirt, the bubbles from his final exhalation and suspends the trail of blood that pours form his head. Even in this apparitional state Santi is anchored within the filthy amniotic fluid of his drowning: his mortal body, dead and still, remains submerged within the depths of the cistern whilst his spirit, alive and moving, is free of the concrete confines of the cistern but still floats within its waters. Even in his spirit manifestation Santi is, once again, positioned as dead and alive, unborn and born, a child of Freud's uncanny womb.

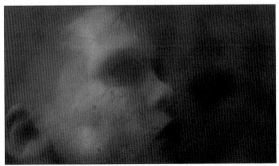

When he manifests himself, Santi embodies the ghost the anonymous narrator spoke of during the film's opening montage: standing within the spectral limbo water, he becomes analogous to the 'insect trapped in amber', a dead being frozen within the transparent material of time. The soft haze that surrounds him evokes the 'blurred photograph' whilst his very entrapment within the water coupled with this spirit's desire for revenge suggests 'an emotion suspended in time', 'an instant of pain' condemned to remain locked in their dying moment.

References

Brinks, E., 2004. 'Nobody's Children: Gothic Representation and Traumatic History in *The Devil's Backbone*', *Journal of Composition Theory*, 24 (2), pp. 291–312.

Blair, A., 2001. *Interview: Guillermo del Toro*. [Online] Available at: http://www.filmsinreview.com/2001/11/22/interview-guillermo-del-toro/ [Accessed 16 October 2008].

Davies, A., 2006. 'The Beautiful and the Monstrous Masculine: The male Body and Horror in *El; espinazo del diablo* (Guillermo del Toro, 2001)', *Studies in Hispanic Cinemas*, 3 (3), pp. 135–47.

Really Scary, n.d. *Guillermo del Toro shows Really Scary The Devil's Backbone*. [Online] Available at: http://www.reallyscary.com/interviewdeltoro.asp [Accessed 16 October 2008].

Endnotes

1   This deathly fate recalls the 1940s/1950s horror tales of EC Comics in which unpleasant characters would engage in a cruel or malicious act and would somehow be punished in an equally cruel and malicious way. Each ending contained a very strong sense of poetic justice, sending out a clear message to the reader – be careful because what you reap is

what you sow.

2   In a slight contradiction to the historic accuracy of the film, del Toro states during his commentary that during the Civil War the bombs that were dropped were not released via the bomb bays as it does in the film. Instead the bombs used were much smaller and were literally dropped out of the plane's windows by the crew.

FILM LANGUAGE – FOCUSED SCENE ANALYSIS

To examine the concept of Film Language, this section will use two interrelated scenes from *The Devil's Backbone*: the first is the seemingly innocuous classroom scene in which Carmen teaches the boys the hunting techniques used by Primitive man and the second scene is the surviving boys attacking Jacinto in the cistern. The connection between the two scenes lies in the image which Carmen shows the boys during the lesson and how this image reverberates into the subsequent violent actions of the boys to make explicit the political dimensions of the film.

Location

The first scene is set solely in a classroom. The *mise-en-scène* – the dirty walls, the peeling plaster and cracked tiles – suggests a state of decay and makes physical Carmen's comments near the very start of the film that the school is so financially impoverished they can barely feed the boys. This decaying quality is emphasised by the soft amber light, the film's visual signifier of death, which fills the room. This light suggests a sense of being frozen in time, of the scene being a moment from the past, a reading which is compounded by Carmen's lesson being concerned with prehistoric history. This sense of the past also functions on an autobiographical level for director del Toro:

> This classroom is visually very much a recreation of the type of classroom I did go to in Jesuit school in Guadalajara in the early Sixties, mid Sixties. These were the type of school benches we had, that's the colour of the walls, the colour of the tile, the type of blackboard, the type of instructional materials. (del Toro, 2004)

In this respect the location clearly correlates with the director's past: it is 'his' classroom the audience are viewing, it is a moment culled from his past that has been physically recreated and presented on the screen. With such an autobiographical location it is possible to connect the protagonists to del Toro also: whilst Carmen talks of hunting mammoths, Carlos and Jaime sit together and talk about writing and drawing fantasy and adventure comics. Given that del Toro is both an artist and a writer, the two boys effectively function as a representation (for only this scene) as a young del Toro dreaming of an adult future in which he spends his days in the fictional realms of fantasy, magic and horror. To compound this reading, del Toro states during his commentary that the sketchbook Jaime draws in during this classroom scene 'is very much based on a diary I keep which is full of drawings and full of ideas. I keep it quite secret and I only make public the parts that concern a particular movie [I'm working on]' (ibid.).

The sole location of the second scene – the cistern – has been discussed at length earlier in this book. To reiterate, the space is a dark and hidden location, one in which a murder has taken place and in which secrets are concealed. Given the narrative

preoccupation with a revengeful ghost, it is essential that the film concludes in the basement of the cistern. In this vaulted cavernous space, the boys confront both the murderous Jacinto and also themselves. By arming themselves and attacking Jacinto, they are crossing the line between child and adult for their actions are with murderous intent. It seems fitting then that such a transition should take place below, in the 'unconscious' space of the cistern.

Costume

Although little can be said about the costumes the actors' wear in both scenes it is important to highlight that the costumes stay the same throughout the duration of the film. Both the boys and Jacinto are seen to be wearing the same clothes throughout the film (a potential period of a few days to a full week passing) and so, again, reinforces the impoverished nature of the school. It is also worth noting that their clothes are of white and cream tones, smeared and marked with dirt. The neutral colours of these clothes do not distract the audience and so allow for their attention to be directed to the faces of the actors. By doing this the age of the children is constantly being highlighted (the young faces against the old, worn and fraying clothes) and constantly juxtaposed against the horrors of the ghost and tyranny of Jacinto's bullying. This also reinforces the hierarchy of age within the school: Carmen and Casares as the elderly parents, Jacinto as the angry young man of the family and the boys as children in an increasingly violent and adult world. Carmen's costume is in contrast to both the boy's clothes and to the classroom itself: wearing all black, she appears as a stark figure against the beige background of the classroom walls. The intensity of the black positions her as a dominating and imposing figure, clearly defining her authority both in the classroom and in the school as a whole. The black also symbolically signifies a sense of loss and mourning, a possible reflection on the death of her husband, Ricardo.

Camera Movement

During the classroom scene the camera is constantly moving: it is either tracking forward towards Carmen or along the rows of the seated boys. These movements primarily add a kinetic dynamic to a scene that is otherwise still – Carmen stands still before the boys whilst the boys themselves are sat still throughout the scene. The camera only stops moving when Carlos and Jaime talk about writing and drawing comics together but even this shot begins with a slow pan up from Jaime's drawing of a mammoth up to the boys' faces.

In the second scene the camera initially continues to move, as it did during the classroom scene, in slow and steady tracking shots. These movements follow Jacinto as he runs down the stairwell into the cistern and then follow him through the space as he looks for the hiding boys. When they confront him with their sharpened stakes the camera abruptly stops moving as if it too has been confronted by the boys and cannot move past the barrier they have created at the edge of the cistern. As the scene progresses all the movement that takes place is by the actors moving in and out of the frame. The camera then remains static, passively observing the violent events unfold.

Editing, Sound and Dialogue

In the two scenes selected for analysis the qualities of editing, sound and dialogue are all interrelated. When combined they direct the audiences attention to certain important aspects of character or action and so preparing them for the emergent friendship between Jaime and Carlos and the conclusion of the film.

The classroom scene is edited as a simple cutting back and forth between Carmen and the boys: Carmen asks the boys a question and so initiates a cut to the boys. When one answers, their dialogue initiates a cut back to Carmen. This process repeats itself throughout the scene until Carlos and Jaime talk but instead of cutting back and forth between these two boys, the dialogue takes place in one long continuous shot, with Jaime out of focus in the foreground. This abrupt stopping of the editing adds a certain type of stillness to the scene and forces audience attention onto the dialogue: Carlos offers to help Jaime write his comics but Jaime responds by saying that they are his and his alone, 'I don't need anyone.' This line of dialogue directly repeats Jacinto's dialogue from earlier in the film for he too says when helped is offered, 'I don't need anyone.' This repetition works to reinforce the parallel/ doubling relationship between Jaime and Jacinto and so suggests that Jaime will soon end up like Jacinto regardless of Carlos' intentions to help him.

It is worth noting that although the two boys sit together in the classroom there is still clear animosity toward each other: when Carlos answers one of Carmen's questions, Jaime retaliates by saying 'your tutor taught you that'. Jaime's dialogue intimates that Carlos has come from a privileged family, one that has enough income to afford for their child to have a tutor. By highlighting this difference the backgrounds of the two boys is subtly hinted at and sets up a further opposition the boys must overcome if they are to become firm friends.

Whilst there is little dialogue during the cistern scene (only Jacinto commenting that the boys are nothing but a joke and Carlos naming Santi before pushing Jacinto into the cistern), the scene itself is a complex combination of editing and sound. As previously identified, the camera stops physically moving moments before the boys attack Jacinto. With a still camera, the boys enter and exit the frame, piercing Jacinto with their spears. The energetic ferocity of the attack is conveyed by the rapid editing from one image to another: a close-up of a spear penetrating Jacinto's arm cutting to a close-up of his pained face cutting to a close-up of one of the boy's, looking down upon him as they raise their spear. The violent intensity of the scene is made all the more evident through the use of close-up, the detail such a composition affords highlighting the pain that Jacinto is feeling. This is most evident in the shot in which Jaime pierces Jacinto in his arm pit – the spear enters into the frame and then enters into Jacinto, all in a lingering close-up that intensifies the physical pain of the injury.

The violence of this framing and editing strategy is amplified by the use of sound. There is only diegetic sound in this sequence and consists of two dominating sounds: the sound of the spears piercing the flesh and the sound of gold 'clinking' in Jacinto's pockets. The 'squelching' sound of Jacinto's flesh being pierced is quite sickening and makes the close-up images of the actual penetration all the more violent and all the more realistic. Whilst these sounds heighten the 'horror' of the scene, the 'clinking' of the gold acts as a reminder to the audience that Jacinto is actually wearing the stolen gold about his person. With such a sound almost consistent throughout the scene, del Toro ensures that when Jacinto is pushed into the water by Carlos that the audience are already aware that the heavy gold will act as a weight, one that will slowly drag him to the bottom of the cistern.

Whilst the attack on Jacinto occurs there is one further diegetic sound present, the music from the gramophone playing in the upstairs room. Throughout the assault the music continues to play, acting as both a 'soundtrack' to the scene and in contradiction to it: whereas the imagery is violent and aggressive, the music is calm and passive and so creating an uneasy juxtaposition between the sound and image. Just as Jacinto is pushed into the cistern, the music comes to end. As stated earlier, Jacinto's character is aligned with that piece of music so, symbolically, when it comes to an end then so should he.

Del Toro has commented on this use of music, stating:

> **We come to the end of the movie and we hear a tango as a background... I have always believed that the tango is the perfect background music to murder and that it truly reflects a side of murder that is often neglected which is passion. (ibid.)**[1]

Within this context, the violence of Jacinto's death is a passionate one, one that expresses the children's desire to avenge not only Santi's death but also Conchita's, hence the lingering close-ups of Jaime's face when he repeatedly stabs Jacinto with his spear.

Iconography

From the political context of the film, Carmen's lesson about how Primitive Man hunted mammoths teaches the boys a valuable lesson in solidarity during conflict. With the image of the hunted mammoth behind her, Carmen says to the boys 'In those days, men had to act in groups. No one could give up.' It is this dialogue that Jaime remembers when the surviving boys are locked in the storeroom: looking at his peers, Jaime walks around them, telling them that they will be killed by Jacinto unless they do something to try and escape. Gálvez argues, pointing out that some of the survivors are injured and, more importantly, that Jacinto has a shotgun and that he is 'bigger and stronger than us'. Before answering, Jaime reaches out and takes hold of a stripped branch and agrees but quantifies his plan by saying 'Yes, but there are more of us.'

In this line of dialogue the power of the group is made blatantly manifest: singular action is useless against an oppressive force. Only through solidarity and group unity can oppression be overcome. In this respect, Jaime applies his understanding of Primitive weaponry (he gets the boys to sharpen the stripped branches with shards of broken glass) and tactics to their situation and understands that they must work as a coherent group if they are to survive. Jaime's galvanising the boys into what is essentially a Republican force (because they are about to come into conflict with the

Nationalist Jacinto) consolidates the film's political message in that the combined force of the group can ultimately overthrow oppression. In the scenes that follow, Jaime's rhetoric as a bully is transformed into the rhetoric of a leader. He organises the survivors, defines roles and actions for them, and, most importantly, maintains the group order and sensibility. He selects group members for their skills and abilities, asking them to play their small part in this much bigger whole. With this strong leader to guide them, the boys successfully lure Jacinto down into the cistern where they attack Jacinto with their wooden spears. Their assault, in its pose, brutality and metaphoric content, reflects almost identically the image Carmen showed the boys during their history lesson. In this context, Jacinto becomes the massive and powerful mammoth that is felled by a group of small boys and their primitive weapons.

References

del Toro, G. (2004). *Guillermo del Toro Commentary. The Devil's Backbone* [DVD]. California: Sony Picture Classics.

Endnotes

1   Del Toro has used the strategy of playing a tango as background music during a murder scene in one of his early shorts, *Dona Lupe* (1985). This film is available on the *Cinema 16: World Short Films* DVD (Region 2).

APPENDIX

The Devil's Backbone and *Pan's Labyrinth*: Further Similarities

- Both films start with a child dying, Santi and Ofelia.

- The antagonist shares the same living space as the children protagonist.

- In both films the young protagonist's biological parents are dead, making them an orphan.

- In both films, the antagonist is a young, handsome and virile male.

- The winding stairs leading down to the cistern in *The Devil's Backbone* are reflected in the winding stairs leading down to the portal to the labyrinth in *Pan's Labyrinth*.

- Keys have an important part to play in both films: in *The Devil's Backbone* Jacinto steals keys to open the safe in order to steal the gold whilst in *Pan's Labyrinth* the key to the storeroom is again stolen, this time by Mercedes. Each of these thefts is a betrayal of trust.

- Jacinto and Vidal both use sex in order to satisfy specific personal needs: Jacinto uses it to steal keys to open the safe; Vidal uses it to gain a son.

- Each film's antagonist is attacked at the narrative's end by a group of people who start off as weak and victimised but, as the narratives progress, grow steadily stronger through friendship, unity and loyalty.

- Both Conchita and Dr. Ferreiro are ordered to obey a command given by the antagonist. When they both disobey they're respective orders they are murdered.

- At one point in each film the young protagonist is chased by a supernatural threat: Santi chases Carlos through the corridors of the school whilst the Pale Man chases Ofelia through the corridors of his banqueting vault.

- In both films there is a character who is missing a leg: Carmen in *The Devil's Backbone* and the Republican who has his leg amputated by Ferreiro in *Pan's Labyrinth*.

Guillermo del Toro Chronology

Born 9 October 1964 in Guadalajara, Jalisco, Mexico. Studies at the University of Guadalajara under Jaime Humberto Hermosillo. Upon graduation he enrols into Dick Smith's Advance make-up course and then sets up his own special make-up effects company, Necropia.

1985	*Doña Lupe*	Director Writer Executive Producer Casting Director Assistant Editor	Short Film
	Obdulia	First Assistant Director	Feature Film
	Dona Herlinda and her Son	Executive Producer	Feature Film
1987	*Geometria*	Director Writer	Short Film
	Love Lies	SPMU FX Artist	Feature Film
1988	*Hora Marcada – Invasión*	Director Writer	TV Episode
	Hora Marcada – Con todo para llevar	Director Writer	TV Episode
	Hora Marcada – Caminos de Ayer	Director Writer SPMU FX Artist	TV Episode
	Goitia, un dios para si mismo	SPMUFX	Feature Film
1989	*Hora Marcada – Hamburguesas*	Director Writer SPMU FX Artist	TV Episode

1990	*Hora Marcada – De Ogros*	SPMU FX Artist	TV Episode
	Hora Marcada – Ángel Pérez	SPMU FX Artist	TV Episode
	Morir en el golfo	SPMU FX Artist Storyboard Artist	Feature Film
1991	*My Dear Tom Mix*	SPMUFX Artist	Feature Film
	Cabeza de Vaca	SPMUFX Artist	Feature Film
	Bandits	SPMUFX Artist	Feature Film
1993	*Cronos*	Director Writer	Feature Film
	Dollar Mambo	SPMUFX Artist	Feature Film
1995	*Algunas nubes*	SPMUFX Artist	Feature Film
1997	Del Toro's father kidnapped. Del Toro and his brothers successfully negotiate his release, which occurred 72 days after his capture. Unwilling to put his family in further danger, del Toro leaves Mexico and moves to the United States.		
	Mimic	Director Writer	Feature Film
1998	Forms *Tequila Gang* Production Company with Rosa Bosch, Laura Esquivel, Bertha Navarro and Alejandra Moreno Toscano. Del Toro's father kidnapped in Mexico. After negotiations he is successfully released.		
	Under a Spell	Producer	Feature Film
2000	*Amores perros*	Editing Supervisor	Feature Film
2001	*The Devil's Backbone*	Director Producer Writer	Feature Film
2002	*Blade 2*	Director	Feature Film
	I Murder Seriously	Executive Producer	Feature Film

Year	Title	Role	Type
2004	*Hellboy*	Director Writer	Feature Film
	Chronicles	Producer	Feature Film
2006	*Pan's Labyrinth*	Director Producer Writer	Feature Film
2007	*Hellboy Animated: Blood and Iron*	Creative Producer	TV
	Hellboy Animated: Sword of Storms	Creative Producer	TV
	The Orphanage	Producer	Feature Film
2008	*Hellboy 2: The Golden Army*	Director Writer	Feature Film
	Insignificant Things	Producer	Feature Film
	While she was out	Executive Producer	Feature Film
	Rudo y Cursi	Producer	Feature Film

Extended Bibliography and Filmography

To help with research, this Bibliography has been divided into the subject areas covered by this study guide. It also contains a considerable number of texts read during the writing of the guide but have not been directly referenced within it.

Films directed by Guillermo del Toro

All films are Region 2 DVD unless otherwise stated:

Blade 2. 2002 [DVD] London: Entertainment in Video.

Cronos. 2006 [DVD] London: Optimum Releasing Ltd.

The Devil's Backbone, 2002 [DVD] London: Optimum Releasing Ltd.

The Devil's Backbone, 2004 [Region 1 DVD] California: Sony Pictures Classics.

Hellboy, 2004 [DVD] London: Sony Pictures Home Entertainment.

Hellboy: The Director's Cut, 2005 [DVD] London: Sony Pictures Home Entertainment.

Hellboy 2: The Golden Army, 2008 [DVD] London: Universal Pictures (UK).

Mimic, 1997 [DVD] London: Buena Vista Entertainment, Inc.

Pan's Labyrinth, 2007 [DVD] London: Optimum Releasing Ltd.

Additional Viewing Material

Dona Lupe, 2008 [DVD] *Cinema 16: World Short Films*, London: Momac Films.

The Orphanage, 2006 [DVD] London: Optimum Releasing Ltd.

The Devil's Backbone

Anon. (n.d.). *Interview with Guillermo del Toro*. [Online] Available at: http://www.esplatter.com/profiles/toro.html [Accessed 16 October 2008].

Blair, A. (2001). *Interview: Guillermo del Toro*. [Online] Available at: http://www.filmsinreview.com/2001/11/22/interview-guillermo-del-toro/ [Accessed 16 October 2008].

Brinks, E. (2004). 'Nobody's Children: Gothic Representation and Traumatic History in *The Devil's Backbone*', *JAC: A Journal of Composition Theory*, 24 (2), pp. 291–312.

Chaw, W. (n.d.). Speak of the Devil's Backbone. *Film Freak Central*. [Online] Available at: http://www.filmfreakcentral.net/notes/speakofthedevilsbackbone.htm [Accessed 16 October 2008].

Chun, K. (2002). *What is a Ghost? An Interview with Guillermo del Toro*. [Online] Available at: http://www.cineaste.com/what.htm [Accessed 15 October 2008].

Davies, A. (2006). 'The Beautiful and the Monstrous Masculine: The Male Body and Horror in *El espinazo del diablo* (Guillermo del Toro 2001)', *Studies in Hispanic Cinemas*, 3 (3), pp. 135–47.

Decapitated Zombie Vampire Bloodbath. (2008). *The Devil's Backbone*. [Online] Available at: http://zombievamp.blogspot.com/2008/02/30-devils-backbone-guillermo-del-toro.html [Accessed 16 October 2008].

Film Freak Central. (n.d.). *Speak of 'The Devil's Backbone'*. [Online] Available at: http://www.filmfreakcentral.net/notes/speakofthedevilsbackbone.htm [Accessed 16 October 2008].

Hardcastle, A.E. (2005). 'Ghosts of the Past and Present: Hauntology and the Spanish Civil War in Guillermo del Toro's *The Devil's Backbone*', *Journal of the Fantastic Arts*, 15 (2), pp. 120–32.

Kaufman, A. (n.d.) *No Mimic: Guillermo del Toro declares his independence with Devil's Backbone.* [Online] Available at: http://www.indiewire.com/people/int_delToro_Guiller_011127.html [Accessed 16 October 2008].

Lázaro-Reboll, A. (2007). 'The Transnational Reception of *El espinazo del diablo*', *Hispanic Research Journal*, 8 (1), pp. 39–51.

Nesbit, J., 2000. *The Devil's Backbone.* [Online] Available at: http://oldschoolreviews.com/rev_2000/devils_backbone.htm [Accessed 16 October 2008].

Pixel Vision. (2006). *Guillermo del Toro on eggs, ghost sightings, lucid dreaming, Catholicism, the 'spuranatural', uterine imagery and more.* [Online] Available at: http://www.sfbg.com/blogs/pixel_vision/2006/12/guillermo_del_toro_on_eggs_gho.html [Accessed 16 October 2008].

Really Scary. (n.d.). *Guillermo del Toro shows Really Scary The Devil's Backbone*, [Online] Available at: http://www.reallyscary.com/interviewdeltoro.asp [Accessed 16 October 2008].

Savage, J. (2002). *The Object(s) of Interpretation: Guillermo del Toro's El espinazo del Diablo.* [Online] Available at: http://www.sensesofcinema.com/contents/02/21/devil_backbone.html [Accessed 10 October 2008].

Selavy, V. (2007). *Guillermo del Toro: Three Twisted Fairy Tales.* [Online] Available at: http://www.electricsheepmagazine.co.uk/features/2007/03/04/guillermo-del-toro-collection [Accessed 16 October 2008].

Smith, P.J. (2001). 'Ghosts of the Civil Dead', *Sight & Sound*, 2 (12), pp.38–9.

Wood, J. (2006). *Talking Movies*. London: Wallflower Press.

Pan's Labyrinth

Guillén, M. (2006). *Pan's Labyrinth – The Evening Class Interview with Guillermo del Toro*. [Online] (Updated 16 December 2006) Available at: http://theeveningclass.blogspot. com/2006/12/pans-labyrinththe-evening-class.html [Accessed 7 November 2008].

Hanley, J. (2007). 'The Walls Fall Down: Fantasy and Power in *El laberinto del fauno*', *Studies in Hispanic Cinemas*, 4 (1), pp. 35–45.

Herrero, C. (2006). *Pan's Labyrinth Study Guide*. [Online] (Cornerhouse) Available at: http://www.cornerhouse.org/ media/Learn/FM%20PANS%20LABYRINTH.pdf [Accessed 11 November 2008].

Janet, J.T. (2008). 'Other Pasts: Family Romances of *Pan's Labyrinth*', *Psychoanalysis, Culture and Society*, 13 (2), pp. 175–87.

Rohde-Brown, J. (2007). 'A Review of *Pan's Labyrinth*', *Psychological Perspectives*, 50 (1), pp. 167–9.

Smith, P.J. (2007). '*Pan's Labyrinth*', *Film Quarterly*, 60 (4), pp. 4–9.

Tanvit, K. (2008). *Pan's Labyrinth of History*. [Online] (Updated 26 Feb 2008) Available at http://blogs.widescreenjournal. org/?p=249 [Accessed 15 October 2008].

Tsuei, K.H. (2008). 'The Antifascist Aesthetics of *Pan's Labyrinth*', *Socialism and Democracy*, 22 (2), pp. 225–44.

Zipes, J. (2008). 'Video review: *Pan's Labyrinth*', *Journal of American Folklore*, 121 (480), pp. 236–40.

The Gothic

Anolik, R.B. & Howard, D.L. (eds) (2004). *The Gothic Other: Racial and Social Constructions in the Literary Imagination*. North Carolina: McFarland.

Baker, B., 2007. 'Gothic Masculinities'. In: C. Spooner & E. McEvoy (eds), 2007. *The Routledge Companion to Gothic*. London: Routledge, Ch. 20.

Botting, F. (ed.) (2001). *The Gothic*. Cambridge: D.S. Brewer.

Briggs, J. (2001). 'The Ghost Story'. In: D. Punter (ed.), 2001. *A Companion to the Gothic*. Oxford: Blackwell Publishing, Ch.10.

Brogan, K. (1998). *Cultural Hauntings: Ghosts and Ethnicity in Recent American Literature*. Virginia: University of Virginia Press.

Castle, T. (1995). *The Female Thermometer: 18th Century Culture and the Invention of the Uncanny*. Oxford: Oxford University Press.

Cavallaro, D. (2002). *The Gothic Vision*. London: Continuum International Publishing Group.

Cornwell, N. (1999). 'Ghost-Writers in the Sky (and Elsewhere): Notes Towards a Spectropoetics of Ghosts and Ghostliness', *Gothic Studies*, 1 (2), pp. 156–68.

Goddu, T. A. (1997). *Gothic America: Narrative, History and Nation*. New York: Columbia University Press.

Grunenberg, C. (ed.) (1997). *Gothic: Transmutations of Horror in the Late Twentieth Century Art*. Massachusetts: MIT Press.

Ellis, M. (2000). *The History of Gothic Fiction*. Edinburgh: Edinburgh University Press.

Hoggle, J.E. (1999). 'Gothic Studies Past, Present and Future', *Gothic Studies*, 1 (1), pp. 1–9.

Hoggle, J E. (2001). 'The Gothic Ghost of the Counterfeit and the Progress of Abjection'. In: D. Punter (ed.) (2001), *A Companion to the Gothic*. Oxford: Blackwell Publishing, Ch. 23.

Hoggle, J.E. (ed.) (2003). *The Cambridge Companion to Gothic Fiction*. Cambridge: Cambridge University Press.

Hopkins, L. (2005). *Screening the Gothic*. Texas: University of Texas Press.

Hurley, K. (2003). 'British Gothic Fiction, 1885–1930'. In: J. Hoggle (ed.) (2003), *The Cambridge Companion to Gothic Fiction*. Cambridge: Cambridge University Press, Ch. 10.

Hurley, K. (2007). 'Abject and Grotesque'. In: C. Spooner & E. McEvoy (eds) (2007), *The Routledge Companion to Gothic*. London: Routledge, Ch. 17.

Kovacs, L. (2006). *The Haunted Screen: Ghosts in Literature and Film*. North Carolina: McFarland.

Miles, R. (2001). 'Abjection, Nationalism and the Gothic'. In: F. Botting (ed.) (2001), *The Gothic*. Cambridge: D.S. Brewer, pp. 47–70.

Punter, D. (1996). *The Literature of Terror: A History of Gothic Fictions from 1765 to the Present Day: Volume 1: The Gothic Tradition*. Essex: Pearson Education Limited.

Punter, D. (1996). *The Literature of Terror: A History of Gothic Fictions from 1765 to the Present Day: Volume 2: The Modern Gothic*. Essex: Pearson Education Limited.

Punter, D. (ed.) (2001). *A Companion to the Gothic*. Oxford: Blackwell Publishing.

Punter, D. & Byron, G. (2004). *The Gothic*. Oxford: Blackwell Publishing.

Sedgewick, E.K. (1980). *The Coherence of Gothic Conventions*. London: Methuen & Co. Ltd.

Smith, A. (2007). 'Hauntings'. In: C. Spooner & E. McEvoy (eds) (2007), *The Routledge Companion to Gothic*. London: Routledge, Ch. 18.

Spooner, C. & McEvoy, E. (eds) (2007). *The Routledge Companion to Gothic*. London: Routledge.

Film Theory

Easthope, A. (ed.) (1993). *Contemporary Film Theory*. Essex: Pearson Education Limited.

Grant, B.K. (2007). *Film Genre: From Iconography to Ideology*. London: Wallflower Press.

Haywood, S. (1996). *Key Concepts in Cinema Studies*. London: Routledge.

Neale, S. (ed.) (2002). *Genre and Contemporary Hollywood*. London: British Film Institute.

Nelmes, J. (ed.) (2003). *Introduction to Film Studies*, 4th edn. London: Routledge.

Psychoanalysis

Easthorpe, A. (ed.) (1993). *Contemporary Film Theory*. London: Longman.

Gay, P. (ed.) (1995). *The Freud Reader*. London: Vintage.

Lear, J. (2005). *Freud*. London: Routledge.

McCaffrey, P. (1995). 'Freud's Uncanny Women'. In: S.L. Gilman, J. Birmele, J. Geller & V.D. Greenberg (eds) (1995), *Reading Freud's Reading*. New York: New York University Press.

Royle, N. (2003). *The Uncanny: An Introduction*. Manchester: Manchester University Press.

Thwaites, T. (2007). *Reading Freud: Psychoanalysis as Cultural Theory*. London: SAGE Publications.

Thurschwell, P. (2000). *Sigmund Freud*. London: Routledge.

Williams, G. (ed.) (2007). *The Gothic*. London: Whitechapel.

Various

Freeland, C.A. (2000). *The Naked and the Undead: Evil and the Appeal of Horror*. Colorado: Westview Press.

Sinyard, N. (1992). *Children in the Movies*. London: B.T. Batsford.